Christlikeness

Christlikeness

Ancient Wisdom for Today's World

Robert P. Vande Kappelle

WIPF & STOCK · Eugene, Oregon

CHRISTLIKENESS
Ancient Wisdom for Today's World

Copyright © 2022 Robert P. Vande Kappelle. All rights reserved. Except for brief quotations in critical publications or reviews, no part of this book may be reproduced in any manner without prior written permission from the publisher. Write: Permissions, Wipf and Stock Publishers, 199 W. 8th Ave., Suite 3, Eugene, OR 97401.

Wipf & Stock
An Imprint of Wipf and Stock Publishers
199 W. 8th Ave., Suite 3
Eugene, OR 97401

www.wipfandstock.com

PAPERBACK ISBN: 978-1-6667-6494-9
HARDCOVER ISBN: 978-1-6667-6495-6
EBOOK ISBN: 978-1-6667-6496-3

12/08/22

Unless otherwise noted, Bible quotations are from the *New Revised Standard Version of the Bible*, copyright © 1989 by the Division of Christian Education of the National Council of the Churches of Christ in the United States of America. Used by permission.

Contents

1. Introduction | 1
2. What It Means to be Christian | 13
3. The Secret Truth Underlying All Theologies | 23
4. The Roots of Christianity | 35
5. Jewish Wisdom Spirituality | 50
6. The Greco-Roman Roots of Christianity | 62
7. The Emergence of Christianity | 79
8. The Pagan-Christian Debate, Part I | 89
9. The Pagan-Christian Debate, Part II | 102
10. A Wisdom Approach to Christianity | 110
11. The Storyline of Stoicism | 122
12. Role Ethics in Stoicism and Christianity | 136
13. The Theological Virtues | 149
14. Returning the Church to Its Roots | 164

Bibliography | 175
Index | 179

1

Introduction

THIS WORLD TEAMS WITH life, thanks to nature and its abundance. The rain falls on every creature, and the sun warms us all. There is a pattern and order to nature that when acknowledged proves to be both generous and hopeful. Humans, following nature, have adopted patterns and rituals that create boundaries and therefore order and meaning to their lives, expressed in families and neighborhoods, societies and nations, and in global citizenship. We have settled into jobs and careers and have devised disciplines, ideologies, religions, arts, technologies, and recreational activities to express our hopes and creative imagination as well as to meet our social, physical, and emotional needs. Life is so good, in fact, that humans have devised ways to enhance and prolong it.

Despite great abundance, nature's goodness seems threatened these days by human waste, negligence, and consumption. If we continue to live arrogantly, selfishly, wastefully, and suspiciously, addicted to violence, chemicals, and hedonistic pursuits, and if we continue to view others as enemies or as inferiors, then the future of humanity and of this planet is bleak. It is not yet too late to change, but if we don't change our attitudes and lifestyles, and do not do so soon, we may reach a hopeless point of no return.

The Good Life

Since the beginning of time, every generation has questioned whether there is a purpose to life, a point to it all. While many people today are skeptical, feeling that life is futile or meaningless, the purpose of religion and philosophy is to posit answers to life's big questions. In a previous book, I pondered this issue and concluded that *the purpose of life is to experience Life, for those who experience life fully experience God, who is Life.*[1] I now wish to modify that statement, adding moral categories to my definition: *The purpose of life is happiness conducive to the equitable flourishing of all, for God is in all.*[2] In what follows I will support the claim that we live in a moral universe and that happiness can be achieved by following specific ethical principles.

Most human beings desire a good life. Thinking about a good life, how to achieve, maintain, and enhance it, occupies a great deal of our time and attention: we build comfortable homes and secure futures for ourselves; we work hard to advance in our careers; we seek to improve our health and expand our minds; we seek satisfying and enduring relationships with people who value similar goals and activities we enjoy. And because we live in community with others, we think about people whose lives have been shaken by war or violence or natural disasters, and we wonder how their needs relate to our lives.

Although Western ethical concerns have traditionally been voiced in Christian language, we know that this search for inner peace, integrity in relationships, and genuine care for other people is widely shared by our neighbors, whether or not they are Christian. While many people today, religious or secular, think of "the good life" in terms espoused by popular culture, namely as a life built around pleasant and interesting experiences, with enough money and leisure to meet personal desires and familial needs, few thoughtful people try to live a good life on entirely selfish terms. In fact, most of our neighbors of other faiths or of no faith would agree that

---

1. Vande Kappelle, *Beyond Belief*, xviii.

2. Though I do not believe in a "personal" God, that is, in a God understandable to human beings and essentially viewed as an "overbig" person, I am not averse to using the term "God." The Bible, both in the Jewish and Christian testaments, declare that "God is Spirit," not person. It was with a metaphysical tradition of personhood in fourth-century Greek theology that calling God "person" took on some meaning. Today, because few of us are metaphysicians of that tradition, we would be better off dropping the notion of the personhood of God and finding a deeper understanding. When we cling to the concept of God as "person," we diminish God's transcendence. Monotheism is to God what a trunk is to a tree. We deceive ourselves if we imagine that the tree is the trunk or that the trunk, being the most visible element of the tree, is therefore the most vital. The tree would be nothing without its roots, which are diverse and rarely visible. In thinking of God, I suggest two metaphors: God is both everywhere to us, like water to fish, but also God is nowhere, like "the void" and "the silence."

Introduction

the good life must include a concern for the well-being of others, peace between nations, and the health of our planet.

For Christians, this general understanding is sharpened by the teachings and example of Jesus, who often took generally accepted obligations and pushed them a step further, beyond what we originally thought. If the teachings of Jesus tell us about what makes a life good, they indicate that it sometimes involves putting the good of others ahead of our own:

> If you love those who love you, what credit is that to you? For even sinners love those who love them. If you do good to those who do good to you, what credit is that to you? For even sinners do the same. If you lend to those from whom you hope to receive, what credit is that to you? Even sinners lend to sinners, to receive as much again. But love your enemies, do good, and lend, expecting nothing in return. Your reward will be great, and you will be children of the Most High; for he is kind to the ungrateful and the wicked. Be merciful, just as your Father is merciful (Luke 6:32–36).

Augustine, in his classic work *The City of God*, imagined humanity divided between two allegiances, one to an earthly or human city and the other to the City of God. The choice between them is absolute, and there can be no middle ground. The two cities are created by two kinds of love: the earthly city, created by self-love, and the City of God, created by the love of God and hence by love for "the Other" (whether conceived as "God," nature, or the stranger in need). In the Bible, the ideal of compassion for the person in need is powerfully illustrated in the parable of the Good Samaritan, found in Luke 10:29–37. Clearly, this business of living a good life is not easy. It cannot be done simply by seeking what is obviously good for oneself. But caring about the good of other people is not simply a matter of helping them get what they say they want. It may involve standing for values that will arouse their misunderstanding and disturb their peace.

Alongside the Christian's love for God, there is the biblical witness that God loves us. The Bible as a whole bears witness to the goodness of creation and its fitness for human habitation. If this is a world created as a place for human life, then our search for a good life has to be shaped in the context of a world that is shaped by love. As Robin Lovin indicates in his primer on Christian ethics, "Belief in God as the creator of a good world is less a narrative of how the world came into being than it is a fundamental confidence that we can live our lives in harmony with the natural world around us.... The search for a good life is not a struggle to wrest peace and happiness from a hostile or indifferent universe. Belief that God has created us for life in this world suggests also that human good is achieved by . . . a common life in which we may achieve a greater good together than any of us controls alone."[3]

Living Virtuously

Humans are happiest when they live virtuously. This is the premise of all of the world's living religions, as well as a core principle in organizations such as the Girl and Boy Scouts of America, among the nation's oldest and most influential youth organizations. Regrettably, this movement is in decline today. However, its principles, as proclaimed in the Scout Oath and in the Boy and Girl Scout Laws, remain untarnished, and if practiced, would impact society profoundly.

Scout Oath: On my honor, I will do my best to do my duty to God and my country, and to obey the Scout Law; to help other people at all times; to keep myself physically strong, mentally awake, and morally straight.

Girl Scout Law: I will do my best to be honest and fair, friendly and helpful, considerate and caring, courageous and strong, and responsible for what I say and do, and to respect myself and others, respect authority, use resources wisely, make the world a better place, and be a sister to every Girl Scout.

Boy Scout Law: A Scout is trustworthy, loyal, helpful, friendly, courteous, kind, obedient, cheerful, thrifty, brave, clean, and reverent.

Many fraternal organizations exist in our world, promoting virtuous behavior. While many members join because they wish to live by high principles and ideals, others join for companionship or to promote agendas for personal success. While it is not always possible to live consistently, in the Bible we find a principle that commends balanced thinking and living. In Matthew 10:16, Jesus exhorts his disciples to "be wise as serpents and innocent as doves." What Jesus meant when he told his followers to live and witness in this manner is the subject of our study.

According to a long-standing tradition in Christianity, there are seven virtues. Four are called "natural" or "cardinal" (the word "cardinal" comes from a Latin word meaning "the hinge on the door"), signifying that they go back to the origins of human civilization and as such are recognized by all cultures as "pivotal" to moral behavior. These four—prudence, temperance,

---

3. Lovin, *Christian Ethics*, 13.

Introduction

justice, and fortitude—represent how human beings can and should behave toward themselves and others. According to Thomas Aquinas, the great medieval theologian, these four virtues God expects us to attain, out of our own human resources. In that respect they represent "natural" human ability at its best.

In 1 Corinthians 13:13, the apostle Paul presents three additional qualities, so eternal and enduring that theologians have grouped them under the category of "theological" virtues: faith, hope, and love. These virtues, transcending ordinary human activity such as devotion, optimism, and kindness, are considered divine gifts for they are viewed as originating with God and as attainable only with divine assistance. Because they are said to come from God, and to distinguish them from natural virtues, we will regularly refer to them as supernatural gifts. Christian authorities believed these virtues were not natural to human beings in their fallen state, but were conferred at baptism.

In later chapters we examine these seven virtues individually and by category, viewing their promissory role as social, moral, and spiritual building blocks, and the theological (supernatural) virtues in particular as symbolic of a deeper metaphysical ontology.[4]

The Law of Love

Morality is often connected with spirituality, and rightly so. Every living world religion acknowledges a natural law, but such law is not the result of

---

4. When we think metaphysically, most of us think dualistically, using paired opposites such as good and evil, light and darkness, male and female, and yin and yang to depict reality, but this way of seeing places limits on our understanding. To expand our horizons, Christian scholar Cynthia Bourgeault suggests that we replace binary systems with ternary perspectives, adding a third "mediating" or "reconciling" principle to the mix. For instance, instead of focusing on man and woman, emphasizing man, woman, and child, and instead of envisioning black or white, seeing black, white, and gray. This principle is evident in the Christian Trinity, with the incarnated Christ as its culminating expression. According to this perspective, the third force is not a product of the first two, as in the classic Hegelian synthesis, but is independent and coequal with the others. The interweaving of the three produces a fourth force or realm of possibility. In contrast to binary systems, which seek completion in stability, through the balance of opposites, ternary perspectives create a synthesis at a whole new level, seeking completion in newness. In *The Holy Trinity and the Law of Three*, Bourgeault advises that we not limit this metaphysical principle to one triad (Father, Son, and Holy Spirit), but rather that we envision the Holy Trinity as one of many triads, each revealing different facets of the divine wholeness.

observation or of mere trial and error. Before there was a universe, there was a benevolent Spirit, graciously loving the emerging cosmos, instilling promise and bringing forth beauty. Ancient Jews and Christians viewed the natural world with awe, affirming it to be God's handiwork.

Because we humans are the product of divine promise, we are happiest when we bring beauty from ourselves and from others, and when we acknowledge and care for cosmic sacredness in its infinite manifestations. We do so best when we live virtuously, energized by faith, hope, and love.

The moral life is not to be lived dutifully or legalistically, but rather graciously, for without grace, all efforts at the moral life collapse. This I have learned from the teachings of Jesus. Because of Jesus, our definition of hero has changed, from flawed warriors and conquering emperors to caring, compassionate individuals. By his embrace of women, children, the poor, outsiders, and other people marginalized by society, and through teachings such as his claim that God knows the number of hairs on our head and his call for shepherds to leave the ninety-nine for the one who is lost, Jesus defied the ancient world to insist that every life matters. In teaching that all people are created equal, Jesus forever offers a better way to cultural superiority and ideologies based on sexism, racism, and classism.

This brings us to a concept that many scholars consider the unifying teaching of the Bible, the moral principle known as The Great Commandment or the "law of love." It was this principle that Jesus both emphasized and exemplified in his ministry, namely, that the fulfillment of moral righteousness depends on the twin commandments of love to God and love to one's neighbor (Mark 12:30–31; Matt 22:37–40; Luke 10:27). This interpretation of the law is echoed by Paul when he says that the whole law is summed up in the single commandment, "You shall love your neighbor as yourself" (Gal 5:14)—or that "Love does no wrong to a neighbor; therefore agape [God's love in us] is the fulfilling of the law" (Rom 13:10). In the Bible, the command about loving God comes first, for it supplies the basis for loving the neighbor.

As followers of Jesus know, the Great Commandment is not a call to "be right" or to a lifestyle built on belief; rather, the Great Commandment is a call to "be in love," a call to a lifestyle built on trust.

When people think of Jesus, some envision God in human flesh; others envision him as an extraordinary or quasi-divine human being; and yet others see him as an imaginary figure, hardly real or historical at all. When I think of Jesus, I see him not as a divine being but as an exemplary person,

Introduction

fully human in that he was able to access human potential completely, utilizing entirely his physical, mental, emotional, and spiritual resources. For that reason we consider him our ideal, for he reflected so faithfully the image of God that he became a bridge to the divine. In that respect he may be considered mentor, master, lord, and savior, truly Emmanuel ("God with us").

As the scriptures indicate, Jesus was completely like us, yet without sin (Heb 4:15), meaning he was one of a very few human beings who perfectly lived out God's will on earth. He was sinless by virtue of never accepting the "lie of separation," which is the core meaning of sin. He could affirm, without hesitation, "the Father and I are one" (John 10:30). He was sinless by living fully out of love, which is God's will for each of us (see Gal 5:6: "For in Christ, neither our most conscientious religion nor disregard of religion amounts to anything. What matters is something far more interior: faith expressed in love," *The Message*). In this light, the phrase "leap of faith" isn't a leap *into* faith but a leap taken because one is already in a trusting relationship with God and wants to put that trust into loving action.

Following Jesus is not a change of *status*—like becoming a member of a club—but a change of *practice*—like a lawyer entering the practice of law, a physician entering the practice of medicine, or an artist entering the practice of writing, music, painting, or sculpture. Followers of Jesus are forever launching into a new way of life, centered on the practice of Jesus' message. The one commonality among Jesus' followers is that they learn through practice.

It is this Jesus I wish to follow, a person whose mindset was rooted in the values of freedom, dignity, and compassion, and who lived to create and maintain an environment where every person, family, and community flourishes fully. This book encourages us to be "Jesus people," imitating the one who lived life fully and authentically, exemplifying what Jesus meant when he told his followers, "I come that you may have life, and have it abundantly" (John 10:10). The mark of the follower of Jesus is not to be a "religious" person but a fully authentic person—open, free, whole, outgoing, compassionate, and a friend to those in need. Followers of Jesus are the ones who can escape the bondage of sin and share life and love unconditionally. They are the ones who have been set free by love. They see this love in the life of the human Jesus and so they call him "Lord" and his way of life "godlike" and "divine."

If discipleship means apprenticeship, then modern disciples of Jesus are called to live radically as "little Christs," modeling their life and

Christlikeness

character on Jesus, their Master and Mentor. If apprenticeship to Jesus is the basic form of God's presence with us, then discipleship entails ongoing openness to God's radical agenda to love and renew the world and all its inhabitants by challenging the status quo, beginning with oneself. In a word, discipleship is "Christlikeness."

The understanding of Jesus' teaching and mission described in this book is revolutionary, inclusive, and controversial. If we should understand Jesus in a nonsectarian way—as neither Jewish nor Gentile, as Paul suggests in Galatians 3:28 (see also 3:7 and Col 3:11)—and the biblical message in a universal way—as a blessing for all peoples and nations of the world and not only for Jews and Christians (see Gen 12:3; Isa 19:24), why did this way of viewing his teaching and understanding his message not have arisen previously?

Many early followers of Jesus did understand that at the heart of his message was the profound and radical idea of God's kingdom (or will) as involving an ethical commitment to God and others rather than a theological solution of the timeless problem of original sin. They also realized that this kingdom was a reality "at hand" and continually with us rather than a going "up" to a timeless heaven after we die. Nevertheless, most Christians living during the ensuing church age came to think more in terms of "us" versus "them" than in terms of "us," more in terms of individual than universal salvation.

There are reasons why the commandment to love God by loving others was missed or overlooked by Christians in the past, but it has little or nothing to do with any notion that modern individuals are smarter or more enlightened than their religious ancestors. In an appendix to his book *The Secret Message of Jesus*, theologian Brian McLaren provides some context and explanation.[5] First, as a result of the missionary efforts of the early church, the Christian movement quickly became primarily a Gentile phenomenon, and after the church's schism with Judaism late in the first century, it came to acquire persistent antisemitic tendencies. Losing the uniquely Jewish dimension of the story of Jesus, the church prioritized theological, christological, soteriological, and eschatological concerns over the essentially ethical nature of Jesus' teachings regarding the kingdom. This narrowing vision also prevented ensuing generations of believers from understanding the radically universal nature of Jesus' message. While the Gentilizing of Christianity led to distortions of Jesus and his message, it

---

5. McLaren, *Secret Message of Jesus*, 211–18.

Introduction

also led to disinterest and ignorance of the first-century setting in which Jesus lived and taught.

The church's early parting with its Jewish roots and Jesus' practical and universal ethical message was also accompanied by a corresponding love affair with Platonic and Neoplatonic forms of Greek philosophy, and their preoccupation with universal rather than particular concepts and timeless rather than timely topics. According to McLaren, such a mindset would predispose readers of the gospels to interpret Jesus' message as "a set of timeless abstractions and miss the historically particular references to contemporary political realities and social movements."[6] As a result, one could very well argue that the excessive time spent by church authorities debating esoteric theological and philosophical issues led to an inordinate dismissal of Jesus' unified ethical vision.

In the fourth century, when Christianity was embraced by Constantine and entered a lasting marriage with the Roman Empire, church scholars and leaders drifted into "safer" abstract readings that didn't question the status quo. Surely there were numerous social, political, and economic advantages—and also liabilities—to the liaison of church and empire. The radicality of what Jesus had envisioned—transformed attitudes, patterns, and lives—was soon watered down by the church, and because Western society was now regarded as Christian, the radical critique of society was largely abandoned.

As Western society came in contact with enemies from within and without, whether violent "barbarians," religious "heretics," or rival cultures and religions such as Islam, the use of violence became endorsed both as a means of propagating and defending the kingdom of God. In such situations, fighting for survival, it was unlikely that the church would consider alternative understandings of Jesus' teaching, even when they were proposed. Ironically, after the Middle Ages, when Protestants broke from Roman Christendom, new church-state liaisons emerged, and Christianity regularly became a servant of nationalism. Even in the period of American independence, Christendom regularly metamorphosed into new forms of civil religion, with most Christian sects and denominations willingly serving the cause of nationalism.

In the eighteenth and nineteenth centuries, during an age of colonization, the Western church in both its Protestant and Catholic forms was energized by an expanding sense of mission. Partnering with colonization,

---

6. McLaren, *Secret Message of Jesus*, 212.

the church discovered, did not lead to new, progressive, or highly reflective beliefs and practices. In addition, colonization—at least in the New World—was accompanied by scandals and atrocities such as the conquest and genocide of Native Americans and accommodation to slavery and racial segregation, and the expanding church in the Western world eventually had to come to terms with byproducts of industrialization and global wars such as environmental degradation, the Holocaust, South African apartheid, and nuclear proliferation. In addition, the Western church had to deal with pedophilia scandals, declining church membership, consumerism, individualism, and the effects of an increasingly secularized society.

What was true for Jesus' contemporaries and for most Christians throughout church history—that they would miss God's kingdom while those from "east and west and north and south" would come and enjoy its benefits (see Luke 13:29-30; Matt 8:11-12)—could certainly be true for adherents to the Christian religion today. Wouldn't it be wonderful if thousands of adherents of Islam, Hinduism, and other faith traditions where fundamentalists and extremists have hijacked religion, begin to take their place in God's kingdom, discovering the underlying message of Jesus in ways that many Christians have not? Could it be that Jesus, recognized as a prophet in Islam or as a messiah by many Jews, could claim the core message of Jesus' teaching as their own? And can't Buddhists, Hindus, and even atheists and agnostics come from "east and west and north and south" and begin to enjoy the benefits of kingdom living, whether they bear the name "Christian" or not? Perhaps the bland religious traditionalism of some Christian churches and the angry, fearful, militant arrogance of others have become sufficiently unattractive that we are closer to a rediscovery of Jesus' transformative message than we might realize? Perhaps just as it took Christianity more than eighteen hundred years to have the courage to face what the message of Jesus meant for slavery, and another hundred to begin to ask what it means for women, and another hundred to begin to ask what it means for the environment—perhaps it always takes time for us to be ready to see the meaning of Jesus' teaching about God's kingdom, a meaning that had been there all along.

In a time of skepticism and unbelief, many voices speak disparagingly of religion. While some of the criticism is deserved, the task of religion continues to be twofold: promoting cohesion and individual identity. At its best, religion promotes the common good by helping human beings live creative, peacefully, and even joyously with realities for which there are no

Introduction

easy explanations. If it is true that there is only one God, as monotheism teaches, then it is both possible and probable that such a God would speak through all the world's scriptures. If "God so loved the world," as the Christian scriptures proclaim, and if this God is acknowledged as Creator of all, then it is altogether likely that this God loves all humans equally.

Perhaps a renewed interest in the nondual social and ethical teaching of Jesus can mark a new chapter in history, the birth of an exhilarating and transformative adventure that could change everything. It is this transformative journey—a new way of thinking and living—that we discuss in the pages ahead.

Questions for Discussion and Reflection

Select one or more of the following questions and write your answer(s) in a journal. If you are in a group study, be prepared to share your answers with those in the group.

1. Do you agree with the premise that life is good? Why or why not?
2. If God can be said to be the ultimate source of goodness, how can this be substantiated?
3. Do you agree that the purpose of life is to find and maximize happiness on planet earth? Support your answer.
4. Do you believe that life has a purpose? If so, write a statement that best summarizes your view or understanding of life's purpose.
5. Do you agree with the author's statement that "Humans are happiest when they live virtuously? Explain your answer.
6. Assess Cynthia Bourgeault's notion that connects spiritual growth or wisdom with cultivating ternary rather than binary perspectives.
7. In your estimation, does the doctrine of the Trinity describe adequately the divine wholeness? Explain your answer.
8. Assess the merit of the author's statement that "human beings are happiest when they bring beauty from themselves and from others."
9. In your estimation, is it possible for people to love others as themselves, as Christ commands? What might the implications of such ways of loving be for people of low or exaggerated self-esteem?

Christlikeness

10. Assess the merit of viewing sin as "the lie of separation." What are the implications of this view for understanding sin and salvation, or for understanding the uniqueness (deity) of Jesus?

2

What It Means to be Christian

IF WE WERE ASKED to classify or describe Christianity, we would probably call it a religion. And we would not be wrong, for Christianity is typically viewed as a religion with three major branches: Roman Catholicism, Eastern Orthodoxy, and Protestantism, the latter further subdivided into many denominations, sects, or ecclesiastical traditions. However, in addition to a religion, Christianity might also be described as a philosophical tradition, a belief system or way of life characterized by moral values and ethical standards, and it is this aspect of following Jesus that I wish to pursue in this book.

While Christianity is best described as a religion, centered upon theological, liturgical, moral, and communal traits and beliefs and exhibiting moral practices and values, it also qualifies as a personal philosophy. In fact, the first Christians were individuals called disciples, a varied group of people with differing political, social, and economic ties united by their belief in and allegiance to Jesus of Nazareth, a wandering peasant teacher whom they admired as role model, mentor, prophet, rabbi, and eventually as master and Lord. Furthermore, in its first centuries, as Christianity grew in size and developed as a movement, it was widely regarded as one of a number of philosophical traditions vying for allegiance in the Greco-Roman world.

What we are discovering today, particularly in the northern hemispheres of our planet, is a crisis in church membership and allegiance, with many members leaving, some switching denominational allegiance and others simply considering themselves as spiritual and no longer as religious, a category often called "nones." Have such people stopped being Christian? In some cases they have, but in most cases they have abandoned Christianity while returning to the values and beliefs of the first followers of Jesus, seeking like them to become "little Christs," that is, truly Christian. Such people know in their hearts the truth of Danish existentialist philosopher Søren Kierkegaard's famous dictum, "It is impossible to be a Christian in Christendom," meaning by "Christendom" a society or nation Christian in name only. As Kierkegaard sensed, only individuals can be Christian, not nations, families, groups, or even ecclesiastical organizations. Like Kierkegaard, Christoph Friedrich Blumhardt, a leader in the Bruderhof Communities, noted that every religion, including Christianity, can become an opponent of Jesus' social and ethical message: "Nothing is more dangerous to the advancement of God's kingdom than religion. But this is what Christianity has become. Do you not know it is possible to kill Christ with such Christianity?"

When we study the history of the Christian religion, we notice a pattern of development that led it far from its roots and from the values, beliefs, and teaching of its founder. In my estimation, Jesus would have been appalled by the requirements and beliefs of the Christian religion that evolved and became attached to his vision and mission. Furthermore, he would have opposed the very notion of the church as an ecclesiastical structure, hierarchically organized and belief-centered. In fact, there is no indication that he wished to create a church or even to abandon his Jewish roots.

At the heart of his teaching was a concept he called the "kingdom (or rule) of God," a way of living, thinking, and being initiated by God and empowered by God's Spirit, a way of life modeled by individuals and leading to communities centered around doing God's will on earth. This kingdom, which Jesus imagined as soon replacing all political, social, and economic structures on earth, would lead to a reversal in attitudes, values, and practices whereby the last—by which he meant the least, the powerless, the poor, the neglected, the outcasts, and the marginalized—would be first. Jesus was calling for a reversal or revolution, not primarily social, political, or religious in nature, but a change of consciousness—from egoic (ego-centered) to unitive (nondual) consciousness—characterized by love of God and neighbor as oneself.

The longer I study church history, the more my views change regarding the institution called Christianity, particularly what we might consider to be its high and low points. In my earlier years, I was enthralled by stories concerning the political change that led Christianity from its minority status to majority status in the Western world. Prior to 312, Christianity had been outlawed and persecuted as antisocial and atheistic for opposing the polytheistic, pagan values of the day. Eventually, under the rule of Roman emperor Constantine, the status of Christians changed from illegitimate to legitimate. Suddenly Christianity was favored and pampered. Constantine thrust it into public life, and the church responded by reimaging its identity and mission. The population of the empire was by no means yet Christian, and paganism did not immediately disappear, but the actions of Constantine decisively placed the imperial power behind the church, with the expectation that the church would also support imperial power.

Succeeding emperors quickly and decisively affirmed Christian privileges, some allowing freedom of worship while others rejected pagan worship and emperor worship. The decisive establishment of Christianity as the state religion of the empire took place under Theodosius the Great, who ruled the east from 379 to 392 and was sole ruler from 392 to 395. By 380, rewards for Christians gave way to penalties for non-Christians. In that year Theodosius issued an edict imposing Christianity on all inhabitants. He closed all pagan temples, where possible converting them to Christian worship. In 392, he declared sacrifice to the gods to be treason, punishable by death. Jews were allowed to assemble for worship, but were not allowed to proselytize or enter into marriage with Christians. Some Christian leaders protested the increasing power of the emperor, implicit in the Christian empire. Theodosius was taking for granted the close link between his own will and God's. The events of the fourth century marked the beginning of Christendom, a socio-political religious movement viewed as the triumph of the Christian religion in the West.

Some have said "the devil joined the church when Constantine became a Christian." A symbol of the times is a Roman coin showing a deity, divine Lord Mithra, but now holding in his hand a cross. Some compromise with culture may seem harmless, such as celebrating Christmas on December 25. This day marked the Roman Saturnalia, a festival celebrating the birth of the sun god. Other mergers with popular custom were more questionable. Once the church had questioned participation in war; now this issue virtually disappeared. Once the church questioned how a rich person could enter the kingdom of God; now the church gloried in its wealth. Pomp and ceremony, modeled in part on that of the state, replaced the simpler worship of the early church. Allied with a hierarchical, imperial government,

Christlikeness

the church reveled in its own hierarchy, removing laypeople from leadership in worship and from government of the church. Indeed, the emperor would issue decrees concerning church government and doctrine.

The most dangerous effect, however, lay in the church's growing worldliness. Once the threat of persecution had weeded out all but the truly committed Christians. Now awareness of the tension between the kingdom of this world and the kingdom of God was fading. Once the lives of candidates for church membership were examined for months before they could be baptized. Soon every subject was expected by law to become a church member.

Beginning no later than the third century, holy men and women dramatically lived out their protest against worldliness. Anchorites retired to the desert to devote themselves to prayer, even seeking physical suffering to put down the flesh. Rejoiced in extreme deprivation, people like Macarius lay naked six months in a swamp, mosquitoes and poisonous insects stinging him nearly to death. Withdrawing from the sinful world to live on top of a column, Simeon Stylites refused to come down even for his own mother's funeral. The "desert fathers" went into the wilderness not to withdraw but to battle Satan. Yet when they felt needed to help the world, some came back. Twice the great ascetic Antony returned from the desert. Once it was to strengthen Christians in persecution. What could the Romans do to him that he had not already done to himself? He came back a second time to defend the faith against Arian heresy. Despite the benefits to Christians enacted by emperors Constantine and Theodosius, I now believe these events mark the nadir or lowest point in the development of Christianity, for they almost completely negated or contravened the values and teaching of Jesus.

While many Protestants might agree with my assessment of the marriage of state and religion under Constantine, Theodosius, and its later permutation in Eastern Christianity under Byzantine emperors such as Justinian, they might strongly disagree with my next lowest point in church history, namely, the Protestant Reformation, particularly its principle of *sola scriptura*, which emphasized the supremacy of scripture as the sole source and rule of Christian faith and practice. Despite the excesses and abuses of the medieval period, including ecclesiastical hierarchicalism, the authority of the pope, the estrangement between laity and clergy, sacramentalism, monasticism, the veneration of relics and saints, the emphasis on good works as meritorious for salvation, and the sale of indulgences, the Reformation contributed to various forms of bibliolatry, a mindset that upholds scripture as sole authority for all Christians but leaves its interpretation to religious and academic experts and ultimately to individual Christians as guided by conscience and God's Holy Spirit. The result was confusion, disagreement, hypocrisy, perfectionism, denominational proliferation, and conflict between Catholics and Protestants, Reform Protestants, and Radical Protestants and ultimately to violence and protracted warfare. In the end, it was obvious that Western Christianity was permanently divided.

Whereas the first low point resulted in abandoning Rome's traditional gods, emperor worship, and many of its pagan rites, it also elevated bishops, archbishops, cardinals, and popes to positions of authority. In fact, many of the rites, practices, and status distinctions that had characterized the imperial cult became perpetuated in the theology and politics of Christendom. Furthermore, despite attempts by individual Reformers and by Reformation movements such as Anabaptists and later by Baptists, Puritans, and Quakers in England and America, many of the rites, practices, and status distinctions that characterized medieval Christendom became perpetuated in the numerous regional and national Christendoms that developed in nation states established by Protestants, particularly under Lutheran and Anglican rule.

The two low points I have mentioned, the first sanctioned by Protestants and the second by Catholics and Eastern Orthodox, are by no means the only ones. Other low points include the Crusades; the Inquisition; the deification of Jesus to Pantocrator status (monarchical role over all authorities on earth, political, religious, and secular); the witch-hunt craze in Europe and Colonial America from about 1450 to 1750; the "five points of Calvinism," which contributed to further divisiveness among Protestants; the elevation of Mary and Christian saints to semi-divine status; promoting status, wealth, possessions, and other aspects of "prosperity gospel"; and the denial of civil rights to women, people of color, and to people of alternative lifestyle and sexual orientation. From what we know of the historical Jesus, he would have opposed each of these elements, practiced and maintained by later Christians in his name.

Developing a Unified View of Reality

In my formative years, both during my formal education and in my early teaching career, I was encouraged to think of my particular brand of Christianity—Protestant, evangelical, Reformed, and conservative—in puritanical ways, namely, as a distinct, pristine, unvarnished, and uncorrupted body of truth that, based on divine revelation, had emerged fully formed and intact from a divinely inspired font of revelation. As a defender and propagator of that truth, found in scripture, it was my task to safeguard its purity from syncretism with or contamination by secular thought and liberal tendencies. The goal was to develop and maintain a unified worldview, based on a biblical view of reality.

How do we develop a unified theocentric view of reality? According to the methodology I learned, the key was to rely on influences from the biblical, patristic, and Reformation periods of church history, for in these phases philosophy and theology were revelatory and God-centered, yielding transcendent standards for human ideas, values, and behavior. Conversely, Christians seeking a unified view of reality should avoid anthropocentric or man-centered thought and activity. The classical Greek Renaissance, and modern eras were portrayed as excellent examples of periods when belief in human autonomy dominated and directed human thought; the contributions of such periods were to be avoided or closely scrutinized, for these periods were characterized by cultural fragmentation and decline.

According to Reformed Protestant thinkers, the ancient Mediterranean world (c. 2000 BCE to 400 CE) presented a sharp contrast between two worldviews, ways of life, or ideals, one biblical and the other pagan or Greco-Roman. Later, during the medieval period (400–1500), a spirit of synthesis or syncretism emerged, in which Christians deliberately attempted to harmonize or unify Christian theology with secular or Greek philosophy. Such cooperation led to the Renaissance and modern eras, a post-synthetic period characterized by the proliferation of new systems of thought inspired by anthropocentric elements such as art, imagination, science, and reason. During the modern and postmodern eras, emerging systems of thought differed radically from the revival of biblical views sparked by the Protestant Reformation, and loyal Christians were called to choose between these two ways of living and thinking, one sacred, theocentric, transcendent, and revelation-based, and the other secular, anthropocentric, humanistic, and reason-based.

Such presentations of reality, highly dualistic, require choosing one system over the other, one divine in origin and ultimately trustworthy, and the other human in origin and ultimately untrustworthy. Since, in matters of faith and practice, we cannot serve two masters, we must choose one or the other, for no synthesis, cooperation, or compromise is allowed. While such one-dimensional allegiance has been required by many churches, cultural, and religious traditions throughout history, no one in modern society lives like that. With some notable exceptions, such as those who withdraw from society and live like hermits or in isolated sectarian communities, the rest of us live in modern comfort, benefitting from advances in science, medicine, healthcare, education, and technology. A dwindling minority, known as fundamentalists, still think dualistically while living and sleeping with the enemy.

Unlike dualistic living and thinking, based on us/them and either/or distinctions, there is a better way, called "second half of life," holistic living, or unitive thinking. Such ways of living and thinking can be fully biblical and yet integrative, inclusive, syncretistic, and synthetic. In a God-infused world such as ours, all things are potentially sacramental and revelatory. As the psalmist declared, "The earth is the Lord's and all that is in it" (Ps 24:1). Starting with that premise, and with the notion that God is sovereign over all creation, we can affirm that God is ultimately in control, governing wisely and lovingly through all genders, races, cultures, and religions. A wonderful truth, attributed to the great medieval thinker Augustine of Hippo and later affirmed by Aquinas, Calvin, and other authoritative Christian theologians, states that "all truth is God's truth." This view expresses confidence in God, truth, the Bible, science, reason, art, imagination, and the ultimate alignment of all inquiry and discovery.

What this comes to mean is that divine revelation comes through many sources. If every human can be said to be a bearer of the divine image (Gen 1:26–27), then every individual, together with every culture, institution, and ideology, can be a conduit or source for truth. Some books, such as those in the Bible, may contain greater or deeper truth than others, just as some people, institutions, and ideologies (social, cultural, philosophical, and religious), may contain greater truth than others, but there is no such thing as pure or untainted truth or revelation. By necessity, all revelation comes through mediation and must be accommodated to limitations in human culture and understanding.

The Bible did not drop straight to earth from heaven, and neither did Jesus. Both came into existence naturally, like other books and other humans. To be human, Jesus was born biologically, like every human, but also spiritually, like every human. Likewise, the Bible was produced by the talent, experience, and imagination of human beings, but also as a result of divine inspiration, much like other great literature. People who are spiritually mature, that is, who are living holistically according to second half of life resources, no longer divide reality into sacred and secular, natural and supernatural, physical and metaphysical, anthropocentric and theocentric, or inspired and uninspired. All things are on a continuum from primitive to complex, immature to mature, ego-centered to other-centered, dishonest to honest, evil to good, false to true, body to mind, and soul to Spirit; and God is in it all!

When Jesus appeared, he taught an ethic based on love of God and of neighbor as oneself. He did not come to convert Jews to Christianity, nor pagans to Judaism, but to transform people from ego-centered to God- and other-centered consciousness, from immature (first half of life) spirituality to mature (second half of life) spirituality, from their False Self to their True Self. He knew he was both human and divine, and asked others to accept their unitive consciousness. Unfortunately, as his followers grew and developed the Christian movement, their desire to create a new religion resulted in great distortions of his meaning, message, and purpose.

For the next fifteen hundred years, Christianity's self-understanding as a philosophy or way of life, a theological and ecclesiastical institution, and an ethical system changed and expanded, until the sixteenth century, when a group of Reformers argued dualistically for a system they called "the three *solas*": *sola* scriptura, *sola* fides, and *sola* gratia (scripture alone, faith alone, and grace alone). By implication, other *solas* were included, such as "Christ alone," "church alone," "Spirit alone," and so on. Of course, to apply the terms "only" or "solely" to multiple beliefs and practices is both ironic and self-defeating. Declared and lived with great conviction, this message changed Europe and Christianity forever, but not necessarily for the better. For such thinking was based on a faulty premise, dualistic and ultimately anthropocentric, like the Romanism they opposed.

The error is in thinking that anything called "*sola*" exists. Scripture, for example, is not "*sola*"; like everything else in reality, scripture is not pure or infallible revelation, but is itself a syncretistic mixture of culture and history, religion and politics, artistry and experience, objectivity and subjectivity, hope and realism. In fact, much of its symbolism, imagery, and wording is taken from pagan neighbors, polytheistic cultures and literature, and "baptized" or made to fit with an evolving Hebraic mindset called "ethical monotheism." Even in Jesus' day, Judaism was evolving and filled with contradictory elements and views. Like the Old Testament, the New Testament also exhibits syncretistic influences and elements, and much of its christological imagery is borrowed from Jewish wisdom literature and pagan and Hellenistic philosophy.

Think of the term "Logos" used of Jesus in the prologue of John's gospel: "In the beginning was the Word [Logos], and the Word was with God, and the Word was God. He was in the beginning with God. All things came into being through him [the Logos], and without him not one thing came into being. What has come into being in him was life, and the life was the light of all people. The light shines I the darkness, and the darkness did not overcome it" (John 1:1–5). While in its New Testament context, these statements can be seen as a commentary on the Jewish creation story in Genesis 1, they are even more appropriately a commentary on Stoic (a pagan Greek philosophical tradition) views of reality. In Stoic thought, the Logos was the divine principle of reason that gives order to the universe and links the human mind to the mind of God. There is nothing in John 1:1–5 that an adherent of ancient Stoicism could not affirm. In fact, properly understood, these verses read as a Stoic manifesto of truth, and therefore as an affirmation of Stoic-Christian compatibility and of the Augustinian maxim, "All truth is God's truth."

Questions for Discussion and Reflection

Select one or more of the following questions and write your answer(s) in a journal. If you are in a group study, be prepared to share your answers with those in the group.

1. Assess the merit of the author's attempt to focus on the ethical rather than on the theological nature of Jesus' message, and on Christianity less as a way of thinking (a dogmatic religion) and more as a personal philosophy or way of life?
2. How do you answer the question, "Can anything take the place of religious affiliation"?
3. Describe the difference between the terms "religious" and "spiritual." If asked to choose between them, which would you select? Why?
4. Assess the merits of Kierkegaard's statement, "It is impossible to be a Christian in Christendom."
5. Assess the merits of Blumhardt's statement, "Nothing is more dangerous to the advancement of God's kingdom than religion."

6. Describe your understanding of the process of changing one's consciousness from an egoic (ego-centered) to a unitive (nondual) consciousness.

7. Assess the validity of the comment that "the devil joined the church when Constantine became a Christian."

8. Assess the validity of the author's comment that adopting the Reformation principle of *sola scriptura* (together with *sola gratia*, *sola fides*, and other *solas*) constituted one of the lowest points in church history.

9. Assess the strengths and weaknesses of developing a way of life based on synthesizing, harmonizing, or integrating religion and philosophy, one sacred, theocentric, and revelation-based, and the other secular, anthropocentric, humanist, and reason-based.

10. Do you agree with the author that developing such a "unified" perspective is essential for the well-being of humanity, the cosmos, and spirituality while affirming God's sovereignty? Explain your answer.

11. Assess the merits of the author's statement that "all revelation [including biblical revelation] comes through mediation and must be accommodated to limitations in human culture and understanding."

3

The Secret Truth Underlying All Theologies

THEOLOGY IS "TALK ABOUT God." The majority of people who use the term "God," particularly in the Western world, have in mind a theistic concept of God, meaning an all-powerful and supreme ruler of the universe. Supernatural theism, by implication, includes the view that all finite things are dependent in some way on this ultimate reality, a reality generally described in personal terms. After all, imaging God as a personal being is very common in the Bible. It is also the natural language of worship and prayer, and there is nothing wrong with it in such contexts. A transcendent reality that does not possess at the very least those qualities that constitute the dignity of human beings, qualities such as intelligence, feeling, freedom, power, initiative, and creativity, could not adequately inspire trust or reverence in human beings. In this sense, God would have to be "personal" to be God. It is doubtful whether believers could worship something that does not have at least the stature of personality.

While the idea of a "personal God" is beneficial in that it makes God relational and accessible to humanity, the extremes of this position, such as presented in the Hebrew scriptures, raise insuperable problems for people in the modern era. This God fights wars and defeats enemies, chooses people and works through them, sends storms, heals the sick, spares the dying, rewards goodness, and punishes evil. Many people have trouble intellectually with these anthropomorphic renderings of God and with the seeming irrationality of belief in a personal God. While only the most traditional believers and the most literal readers of scripture believe such things anymore, this deity remains the primary object and substance of the Christian church's faith. It is this understanding of God that is becoming meaningless to increasing numbers in the modern world.

While it is attractive to speak of intimacy with God and accessibility to God, religious philosophers have long warned against ascribing human qualities and attributing human feelings to God. Still, the joy of familiarity with God and the need to recognize and be recognized by God override the philosopher's critique. There is, however, a critical flaw in this perspective: Once we conceive of God as a person like ourselves, God becomes open to criticism.

To protect God, apologists and theologians urge us to discard this way of thinking. God is not like us, says twentieth-century theologian Karl Barth; God is "Totally Other." This understanding views God as different not only in degree but also in kind. Humans can only speak of God indirectly, says thirteenth-century theologian Thomas Aquinas, for they cannot "know" God directly. Humans can only speak of God or "know" God indirectly, by saying what God is not (the *via negativa*), or by saying what God is like, thereby resorting to analogies or metaphors (the *via analogia*).

In using models of transcendence, whereby God is said to be all knowing, all powerful, and all good, we instinctively know that we are not referring to the same kind of qualities we understand when speaking of attributes in humans. Does this mean, then, that God cannot be said to be moral in the manner that we are said to be moral? If so, that raises deep resentments. We hear it in the outburst of the philosopher John Stuart Mill: "I will call no being good who is not what I mean when I apply the epithet to my fellow creatures, and if such a being can sentence me to hell, to hell I will go."[1] In his publication, *The Sins of Scripture*, Bishop Spong examines biblical moral principles attributed to the will of God and concludes that those who wish to base their morality literally on the Bible have either not read it or not understood it.

As Rabbi Harold Schulweis observes, "In elevating God to the level of transcendent lawgiver and judge, the human being is drawn increasingly subordinate to the will of God. An alienating dualism has intruded in the original picture, splitting the divine and the human, erecting a wall between God 'above' and nature 'below.' As a result, questions about prayer, miracles, and revelation are turned into forced either/or options. Prayer is either a unilateral response from God or a lonely human monologue;

---

1. Cited by Schulweis, *Those Who Can't Believe*, 132.

The Secret Truth Underlying All Theologies

miracle is either God's intervention or human invention; revelation is either God's word cast down from above or a soliloquy from below."[2]

But what are the alternatives? Is atheism (a-theism) the only alternative to theism? Technically, of course, there are numerous options, including polytheism (the belief that there are numerous deities), pantheism (the belief that God is in everything for everything is divine), henotheism (the notion of worshipping a territorial god, conceived as one god among many), animism (the belief that nature is filled with spirits or souls, which must be worshipped or appeased), and panentheism.

Many people today are finding the case for panentheism increasingly attractive in an age of science and reason. One can find historical traces of panentheism in both western and eastern orthodox theology, though the word itself was popularized by English philosopher Alfred North Whitehead (1861–1947). Panentheism is not the same as pantheism, the concept that "all things are God." Rather, pan*en*theism is the concept that "all things are *in* God." Panentheism views God not as a supernatural being separate from the universe, beyond nature and history, but as the encompassing Spirit around us and within us. According to this conception, God is more than the universe, yet the universe is in God. Viewed spatially, God is not "out there" but "right here." Whereas supernatural theism emphasizes God's transcendence—God's otherness, God as more than the universe—panentheism affirms both the transcendence and immanence of God. It does not deny or subordinate one in order to affirm the other. For panentheism, God is both more than the universe and yet everywhere present in the universe.

Fortunately there are alternatives to the concept of theism, for "theism" and "God" need not be the same. Supernatural theism is but one human definition of God. Panentheists affirm that "God" does not refer to a supernatural being "in heaven," apart from nature, but rather to the sacred at the center of existence, the holy mystery that is around us and within us. Panentheism affirms the centrality of mystery in the universe and the possibility of relating intellectually and experientially to that mystery. It is possible, then, to be an agnostic or even an atheist regarding the God of supernatural theism and yet be a believer in God in the way offered by panentheism.

In his accessible book titled *The God We Never Knew* (1998), biblical scholar Marcus Borg examined the variety of images of God in the biblical and Christian traditions and discerned therein two primary "models":

---

2. Schulweis, *Those Who Can't Believe*, 132.

Christlikeness

1. The *"monarchical model,"* which clusters images of God as king, lord, and father. This approach leads to what Borg calls a "performance model" of the Christian life.

2. The *"Spirit model,"* which clusters images of God that point to intimate relationship and belonging. This model leads to a "relational model" of the Christian life.

Both models, Borg discovered, are found throughout all periods of Christian history, though the first is more common. From roughly the fourth century—when Christianity became the dominant religion of Western culture—through the present, the monarchical model has dominated. But alongside it, as an alternative voice, the Spirit model has also persisted. These models reflect two different voices within the Christian tradition.

The monarchical model portrays God as male, as all-powerful, as lawgiver, and as judge. Images of God in this model suggest that God is distant. Within this model, humans have offended divine majesty and deserve judgment. But because God loves his subjects, God creates a way for his people to escape the punishment they deserve: through appropriate sacrifice and true repentance. In the royal theology of ancient Israel, atonement was institutionalized in temple rituals. In the Christian version of the monarchical model, the king's (Lord's) love is seen especially in Jesus. Because God loves us, he sends his son into the world to die on a cross as the sacrifice that makes our forgiveness possible.[3]

The Spirit model, as used in the Bible, is broader than the specific Christian doctrine of "the Holy Spirit," which sees the Spirit as one aspect of God. In the Bible, Spirit is used comprehensively to refer to God's presence in creation, in the history of Israel, and in the life of Jesus and the early church. While the monarchical model also affirms that God is Spirit, of course, and that affirmation can be a source of confusion that limits our understanding of God, there is a difference. When Spirit is assimilated to the monarchical model, God is not Spirit but a spirit—that is, a spiritual being out there, not here. But when Spirit is set free from the monarchical understanding, Spirit retains the suggestive meanings associated with breath and wind: God is the encompassing Spirit both within and outside us.[4]

In addition to wind and breath, the Bible provides other non-anthropomorphic images, such as rock (meaning a place of refuge and safety).

---

3. Borg, *God We Never Knew*, 63–64.
4. Borg, *God We Never Knew*, 72.

Additional non-masculine images include mother, wisdom, lover, and shepherd. These metaphors for the Spirit affect our root image of God in quite obvious ways: (1) they emphasize *the nearness of God* rather than the distance implied by the monarchical model, thereby suggesting the language of relationship; (2) they utilize *both male and female metaphors* (as well as some that are neuter), rather than the exclusively male images of the monarchical model; and (3) they include *both anthropomorphic and nonathropomorphic images*. Taken together, both models suggest that the relationship to God is personal, even as God is more than a person. The sacred is not simply an inanimate mystery but a presence. Using an ancient biblical analogy, these metaphors lead to a covenantal understanding of the divine-human relationship, which emphasizes belonging and connectedness. This model is intrinsically dialogical.[5]

The Spirit model of God affects the meaning of a number of central Christian teachings. It does so by changing the framework in which things are seen. Borg provides four examples:

1. *Creation looks different*. According to the monarchical model, God's creation of the world is understood as an event in the distant past involving the creation of a universe separate from God. The Spirit model depicts God's creation as an ongoing activity: in every moment God as Spirit (as the nonmaterial "ground" of all that is) is bringing the universe into existence.

2. *The human condition looks different*. Our central problem is not sin and guilt, as it is within the monarchical model, but "estrangement," meaning that humans are separated from that to which they belong. Our problem is blindness to the presence of God, separation from the Spirit that is all around us and within us and to which we belong.

3. *Sin looks different*. For the monarchical model, sin is primarily disloyalty to the king, seen especially as disobedience to his laws. The Spirit model addresses "sin" is more profound ways: for the metaphor of God as lover, sin is unfaithfulness; for the metaphor of God as the compassionate one who cares for all her children, sin is failure in compassion. Thus sin remains, but as betrayal of relationship and absence of compassion. Repentance also remains, only now it does not require sacrifice and contrition but a turning and returning to that to which we belong. Judgment also remains, only now not as the threat of eternal

5. Borg, *God We Never Knew*, 75–76.

judgment but rather as living with the consequences of our choices. To remain estranged from God is to remain unsatisfied and unfulfilled.

4. *God as king and lord looks different.* God as Spirit is glorious, radiant, and splendid, like the splendor of a king. In the Spirit model, God as king and lord is the subverter of systems of domination, not the legitimator of domination systems.[6]

The images of God associated with the Spirit model dramatically affect how we think of the Christian life. Rather than God as a distant being with whom we might spend eternity, Spirit—the sacred—is right here. Rather than sin and guilt being the central dynamic of the Christian life, the central dynamic becomes relationship—with God, the world, and each other.

The mystics of every religious tradition, following the Spirit model rather than the monarchical model, have always spoken out against specific definitions of God. The Western mystics appear to have assumed that a personal God was only a stage, and an inferior one at that, in human religious development. The mystical portrait of God was first imaginative, and then ineffable. It involved an interior journey, not an exterior one. In the mystical tradition no one can claim objectivity for his or her insight. Each person is called to journey into the mystery of God along the pathway of his or her own expanding personhood. Every person is thus capable of being a theophany, as sign of God's presence; but no one person, institution, or way of life can exhaust this revelation. God, for the mystics, is found at the depths of life, working in and through the being of this world, calling all nature to its deepest potential.

Religion as Noun or as Adjective

When modern Western people think about religion, they mostly view it as a noun, describing distinct social bodies or as an adjective describing an attitude toward the human condition—a way of seeing, acting, and experiencing reality. Throughout history most people thought of religion as an adjective and not as a noun, as a separate reality they had to choose over and against another reality. The first approach, treating the word religion as a noun leads each person to understands himself or herself as identifying with and belonging to only one of those organization. For example, if you are a Christian, you are by definition not a Jew or a Buddhist. But this

6. Borg, *God We Never Knew*, 77–78.

way of understanding would be foreign to a person living in antiquity, and today it is foreign to many people living in Africa and Asia. In Japan, for instance, it is possible to be Buddhist, Taoist, Confucian, and Shinto all at the same time.

Unlike most adherents of Western religions today, ancient Greeks and Romans viewed religion as a way of respecting all powers, natural and supernatural, that govern one's destiny, whether they be associated with war, fertility, or other aspects of society. Naturally, one would want all those forces on one's side. Anything else would be disastrous. For ancient Romans, as for nearly all other people throughout history, religion was essentially about divine favor and its influence on human destiny. According to this primal perspective, religion is not just about "spiritual" things, or deities, or God. Rather, religious attitudes are as diverse as the forms of power that people believe govern their destiny, whether these forms of power are related to nature, wealth, political power, individual well-being, or the forces of history.

In light of primal spirituality, the contemporary tendency to think of religion as a noun is rather unique to the contemporary Western world, for such a view represents a departure from what has been commonly understood by most people throughout history. Also, reframing religion as an attitude toward power, an attitude that includes social, political, and economic power, suggests that religion must be understood as a phenomenon pervading all of society, rather than as a distinct element existing in but separate from other elements of society.

Thinking of religion and spirituality as nouns is exclusive and highly dualistic, for it places a wedge between people and forces them to choose between competing alternatives. However, if we think of religion as an adjective, shifting from distinct social groupings to a universal human way of seeing, acting, and experiencing reality, we provide a way of viewing reality that is more inclusive and nondualistic.

Likewise, when modern Western individuals think about God, they think in terms of monotheism—primarily of the exclusive and highly dualistic view of God we are calling supernatural theism. As we noted earlier, those who adopt this way of thinking about God limit the alternatives to four: if one is not a monotheist, then one is either a polytheist, a pantheist, or an atheist. To that we must now add a fifth possibility, namely panentheism.

While it is possible to approach views of God's nature and existence from an exclusively subjective perspective—arguing that spiritual reality and truth are strictly matters of opinion and that all such views are equally valid—what if we were to affirm the principle, "Go deep in any one perspective and you find universal truth"? According to this view, the following implications appear valid, namely, that (1) truth is both subjective and objective, (2) there are factual elements (elements of nonfiction) in all fiction, and (3) there are fictional elements in everything we call fact, dogma, doctrine, religion, ideology, and points of view. The implication of such views in theology ("God-talk") seem to lead naturally to the view espoused by novelist Marion Zimmer Bradley in her bestselling novel of Celtic spirituality entitled *The Mists of Avalon*. In her view, the Arthurian legends represent a coming together of two traditions, Celtic pagan and non-Celtic Christian traditions, an amalgam not unlike the earlier Canaanite pagan and Israelite traditions, or the later Judeo-Christian and Greco-Roman synthesis, a view she expresses in her famous dictum: All the Gods are one, and all the Goddesses one, and the truth is within. The solution to holistic living is balance, moderation, and the equality of all in a world ruled by love. As Bradley states, using Merlin, the legendary Wizard, as mouthpiece, "I think you mistake the nature of Heaven . . . Do you really think mankind's quarrels and imperfections will be carried on in Heaven? . . . I have one thing in common with (Christian) priests. I have spent much time trying to separate the things of man from those that belong to the Divine, and when I have done separating them, I find there is not so great a difference. Here on Earth, we cannot see that, but when we have put off this body we will know more, and know that our differences make no difference at all to God."[7]

According to this perspective, God appears to each of us as we can best understand God. In the end, divine will trumps all human effort, leading to the great ethical ideal, "Love all and harm none; that is the whole of the law."

Power Shared: Affirming the Big Truth

Throughout much of Western history—certainly since the time of Constantine, well into the Enlightenment period, and, in some cases, to the present—Christianity has thrived in a culture of domination and supremacy, be it under Roman Catholicism, Protestant versions of Christendom, even Puritan versions of religious liberty. Why is this so? Why have Christians turned God into an omnipotent sovereign "Lord," Jesus into "Christ the

---

7. Bradley, *Mists of Avalon*, 37–38.

King," and the Holy Spirit into an agent who guides only select individuals into eternal, unchanging truth?

The Christian Trinity, properly understood, stands for the exact opposite, a loving, relational entity who flows through all things since the beginning. We fail to understand Jesus and the Holy Spirit if we don't first participate in the eternal dance of mutuality and communion within which they participate. Like the being we call God, Father, or Mother, Jesus and the Spirit dwell in a realm of love, grace, and abundance, not in a realm of domination.

Christians need to let go of their pyramids of power, of their empires, wealth, patriarchy, and control. If Western Christians surrendered their false dualistic models of truth, reality, and relationality to nondualist Trinitarian models, their notions of society, politics, and authority would utterly change—from top-down and outside-in to grass-roots spiritual patterns and norms. Circles, ellipses, and parabolas are far less threatening to individuals and communities based on the wholeness and inclusivity modeled by Jesus.

Unfortunately, it took early Christians less than three centuries, in some cases less than a century, to transform the one who described himself as "gentle and humble in heart" (Matt 11:29)—one described by the early church as having displayed kenosis[8] by humbling himself to the point of death on a cross (Phil 2:8)—into an imperial deity, both in Western (Roman) Christianity and in Eastern (Byzantine) Christianity. When the Roman Empire converted to Christianity, the Greek Zeus (Roman Jupiter) became the Latin *Deus*, the vulnerable, relational, kenotic Jesus became unrecognizable, and the Christian Trinity became imperial, totalitarian, and fearsome.

The Christian Trinity, however, is just the opposite, for, as Jesus taught—in word and through example—God's power is not dominating, threatening, or coercive. Paul, too, was faithful to the original message, telling the Corinthian believers that "when I am weak, then I am strong" (2 Cor 12:10), learning this lesson by revelation from Jesus, who declared for all time the sacred lesson that "power is made perfect in weakness" (2 Cor 12:9), a self-emptying truth Jesus modeled persuasively on the cross.

This, then, is how God creates, and how God rules. God's creative "Let It Be" approach should be ours as well, for all who believe and love

---

8. Kenosis is the concept of willful self-emptying in order to become entirely receptive to the divine will. An aspect of the incarnation of Christ, kenosis involves the relinquishment of divine attributes by Jesus Christ in becoming human.

God are called to be co-creators in God's eternally unfolding promissory potentiality. "The grace of the Lord Jesus Christ, the love of God, and the communion of the Holy Spirit" (2 Cor 13:13) should be the nondualist and inclusive ecology for all we do and for how we do it, including how we display power, mercy, and justice.

Divine power is shared power, gracious and free. If there is no self-serving domination in the Triune God, how should we, God's children, view power? In her 2018 book *Dare to Heal*, Brené Brown distinguishes between "power over" and "power with." While there is no "power over" in the Trinity, there is empowerment, that is, "power with"—a giving away, sharing, letting-go sort of power, and thus an infinite flow of trust and mutuality. Instead of empowering, self-giving power—in marriage, in culture, and in international relations—Christians have traditionally preferred rulers, empires, wars, and domination. This form of human power, modeled in patriarchal, imperial, and ecclesiastical domination systems, is a perversion, a masquerade of divine power. For "in Christ Jesus . . . the only thing that counts is faith working through love" (Gal 5:6). In Jesus, God models power, and it ends up being vulnerable, humble, and self-giving. How different this is from the "rights" that shape the American national identity, with its rights to "life, liberty, and the pursuit of happiness." So much of American history, by contrast to the values espoused by Jesus, consists of groups of individuals protecting themselves and what is theirs with a gun, a flag, or the cloak of racial, class, or gender privilege.

When we take something we possess—our wealth, our power and influence, our comfort and control, our society and institutions, even our identities and abilities—and make them useful to others, we are practicing kenosis, a powerful and creative form of spirituality.

For much of the first millennium of Christianity, Christian scholars used the word "catholic" to define the church and its unifying truth. According to Vincent of Léarins (died c. 450), a central feature of the church's universal nature, message, and vision lies in holding "fast to what has been believed everywhere, always, and by all."[9] In other words, if something is true, then it must be true everywhere and at all times.

Unfortunately, throughout history human beings have often preferred local truths such as cultural truth, denominational truth, national truth, scientific truth, rational truth, factual truth, and personal truth, dualistic views contrary to mature spirituality, which affirms the Big Truth beyond

---

9. Morris, *Fathers of the Church*, 270.

these limited truths. This is what makes authentic spirituality inherently subversive and threatening to all systems of power and control. Holistic spirituality always says, "Yes, and."

Such recognition of power and authority beyond one's own group is demanded of Christians by the fact that their Bible includes the Hebrew Bible. Think of this for a moment; inclusivity is valued and demanded from the start. Every Christian liturgy acknowledges as authoritative texts from the Torah, the Jewish prophets, and Jewish wisdom literature. Christians include Abraham, Moses, and Elijah as their spiritual ancestors, yet none of them knew Jesus or were Christian. The implications should be clear: Christians have been taught by non-Christians from the beginning. The door to otherness is open and must remain open lest Christians become insular instead of "catholic."

As noted earlier, the pattern continues with John's gospel using the concept of the Logos, which was first used by the pre-Socratic Greek philosopher Heraclitus and later by Greek Stoic philosophers. Paul, too, quotes non-Jewish sources and worldviews to the Athenians (Acts 17:26–29) in order to proclaim a more universal message. Likewise, early church theologians such as Clement and Origen of Alexandria relied upon "pagan" philosophers to make Christian points, as did Augustine with Plato and Aquinas with Aristotle. This, then, is the Christian heritage, using universal wisdom to teach Christian doctrine. As great Christian thinkers readily acknowledge, no single individual or group can ever encompass the magnificent and always mysterious teaching of Jesus regarding the nature and rule of God.

Questions for Discussion and Reflection

Select one or more of the following questions and write your answer(s) in a journal. If you are in a group study, be prepared to share your answers with those in the group.

1. What is your understanding of God? Do you view God as personal, impersonal, or as both? Support your answer.
2. Can people worship God or even relate to God meaningfully apart from a "personal" (theistic) understanding of God? Explain your answer.

3. In a few sentences, define panentheism. How does this view differ from theism? Why is this approach to God becoming increasingly attractive to people today? Assess the merits of this perspective.

4. Which of Borg's two biblical models for God do you find most attractive, the "monarchical" or the "spirit" model? Must we choose between them? Is there a better model?

5. In your estimation, how does the panentheistic or Spirit model of God change the way you view nature?

6. In your estimation, how does the panentheistic or Spirit model of God change the way you view the human condition?

7. In your estimation, how does the panentheistic or Spirit model of God change the way you view sin?

8. In your estimation, how helpful is the author's distinction between speaking of religion as noun or as adjective? Which approach do you favor? Why?

9. In your estimation, is it possible for American Christians to substitute their culture of domination and their theology of supremacy for a culture and theology of shared power? Explain your answer.

10. What would it mean for Western Christianity to base its spirituality and way of life on the practice of kenosis?

4

The Roots of Christianity

CHRISTIANITY IS ESSENTIALLY A historical religion. It cannot be understood simply through a set of dogmas, a moral code, or a view of the universe. For through the stories of Israel, Jesus, and the developing church, Christianity acknowledges the revelation of God in action. As an institution, the church has an identity and a mission, and as an organism, it necessarily develops from infancy to maturity, undergoing the growing pains of adolescence, young adulthood, and midlife as well as periodic transformation due to changing cultural needs and challenges.

It is important to remember that when anyone—politician, social activist, or church reformer—calls for a radical new start, a complete break with the past, he or she is shooting at the moon, for no clean break with the past is possible. Every generation, just as every individual, is the result of the subtle yet dominant influences of the past. The philosopher Bertrand Russell claimed that one of the great faults of the twentieth century was that it limited itself to a "parochialism in time," viewing the old as antiquated and irrelevant and only the new as pertinent. Lord Acton made the same point: "history must be our deliverer not only from the undue influence of other times, but from the undue influence of our own."

History, then, has to do with the study of the "otherness" of the past. It involves trying to allow that "otherness" to speak to us. If we are to be liberated from the tyranny of the present, we must try to see life with the eyes of centuries other than our own. In that way we embrace the past in the present. We must allow individuals of the past to pose their own questions rather than imposing upon them our own fascinations, hopes, and neuroses. Only in this way will the study of the past open up to us a larger present.

Another benefit from the study of the past is its usefulness in shaping proper attitudes toward scripture. While Christians value the Bible, they do not always agree on its message. Studying the history of Christianity provides perspective on the interpretation of scripture, for it acquaints us with vast differences in how the Bible has been used and understood. Because its members and leaders are human, the church is not perfect, as its history makes abundantly clear. For that reason, the study of church history should increase our humility about who we are and what we believe. In addition, historical study helps us distinguish between biblical chaff and wheat, preserving our deepest commitment only to those aspects of Christian faith that deserve such commitment, while enabling us to act with even greater toleration in a cultural climate becoming increasingly diverse.

While many Christians value the study of church history, some disparage it as unnecessary and irrelevant to their spiritual well-being. Unlike traditional Roman Catholic or Eastern Orthodox Christians, who value tradition, evangelical Christians typically go directly to scripture for guidance or inspiration, neglecting the value of tradition for faith and practice. They often appeal to Martin Luther and other Protestant Reformers, who argued for the primacy of scripture above all other authorities.

When Protestant thinkers such as Martin Luther coined the phrase *sola scriptura*, establishing the Bible as the source and sole authority of their faith, they were protesting the role of tradition—particularly the medieval accretions that defined Latin Christianity—as equally binding. Their methodology, encapsulated in the phrase *ad fontes* (back to the sources), defined their strategy. They believed the scriptures, practically and clearly interpreted, to be adequate and sufficient for faith and practice. In addition, they argued, the church stood in need of purification from excessive reliance upon secular medieval institutions and practices such as state, culture, philosophy, and reason. Rejecting the synthesis mentality of the thousand-year-old Holy Roman Empire, which valued equally scripture and tradition, the Protestant Reformers attempted to return to an undiluted biblical way of thinking, without realizing that the scriptures upon which they were relying also included a synthesis mentality, as yet undetected. Unfortunately, the Reformers' search for purity resulted in the further fragmentation of Christendom, first into four sectarian bodies (Lutheran, Reformed,

Anglican, and Anabaptist), and eventually into hundreds of denominations and thousands of sects.

The first Christians lived in a Greek world, dominated by diverse values and beliefs. As Jews, they drew on Hebraic customs and beliefs, themselves shaped by alien cultural influences: Sumerian, Amorite, Egyptian, Hittite, Phoenician, Aramean, Assyrian, Babylonian, and Greek. Over time, these and other ancient neighbors in the eastern Mediterranean world had supplied beliefs and practices that resulted in views of God grouped variously under the rubric called ethical monotheism. Like their forebears, the first Christians tried to reconcile diverse visions of deity, and the results, far from uniform, elicited unstable answers to unending questions.

The Emergence of Monotheism

The principal figure in the Bible—as in life—is God, and the central theme of the Bible—as of all mystical experience—is the relationship between humans and God. But when Jews worship, which God do they worship? The radical God of Abraham, the capricious God of Sarah, the legalistic God of Moses, the nationalistic God of David, the exclusive God of Isaiah? How about Christians? Do they worship the surprising God of Mary, the empowering God of Peter, the sentimental God of Mary Magdalene, the loving God of Jesus; the mystical God of Paul, the orthodox God of Augustine, the impassive God of Aquinas, the gracious God of Luther, the sovereign God of Calvin, the puritanical God of Jonathan Edwards, the just God of Martin Luther King, the redeeming God of Billy Graham, or the progressive God of Pope Francis? While the explanations for the varied views of God held by these individuals are historical, linguistic, social, cultural, and theological, they are also biblical.

When Karen Armstrong, former Catholic nun and now leading religious scholar, began to research the history of the idea and experience of God in the three Abrahamic faiths (Judaism, Christianity, and Islam), she was surprised to discover that eminent monotheists in all three traditions, instead of advising devotees to wait for God to take the initiative in the relationship, encouraged them to create a sense of God for themselves. Some spiritual masters discouraged believers from expecting to experience God objectively, as a reality "out there," suggesting that in an important sense God was a product of the creative imagination. A few highly respected monotheists, thinking philosophically, denied God's existence while emphasizing that God was the most important reality in the cosmos.[1] While ideas like these boggle Western rationality, such paradox is central to authentic spirituality.

Historically speaking, there is no one unchanging idea in the word "God"; instead, the word contains an entire spectrum of meanings, some of them contradictory and even mutually exclusive. Indeed, the statement "I believe in God' has no objective meaning, but like any other statement only means something in context. The same is true of atheism. Since one cannot logically say for certain that there is no God, people dubbed atheists usually deny particular conceptions of the divine. Had the notion of God not had sufficient flexibility, it would not have survived to become one of the great human ideas.

Building on the contributions of dialectical philosopher Georg Wilhelm Friedrich (1770–1831), evolutionary scientist Charles Darwin (1809–1882), and cultural anthropologists Sir Edward Tylor (1832–1917), critical religious scholars of the nineteenth century considered it axiomatic that all religions go through evolutionary stages of development, moving from the simple to the complex. When the distinguished German biblical scholar Julius Wellhausen (1844–1908) examined the stories and laws that appear in the Hebrew scriptures, he concluded that Israelite religion evolved in stages from primitive animism to ethical monotheism. Critical scholars have detected as many as five such stages:

- Animism—belief that all natural objects are inhabited by souls. While enhancing awareness, in this phase religious attention is directed toward appeasing these souls. Hints of this mindset have been found in the talking serpent of Genesis 3, in Abraham's conversing with angels by the oaks of Mamre in Genesis 18 (some scholars suggest that Abraham may have been communicating with spirits that inhabited the trees), in Jacob's visions of a heavenly ladder while sleeping on a stone pillow at Bethel (Gen 28:18 suggests that the stone became a cult object), and in the commandment to make altars only from uncut stone (Exod 20:25), supposedly to avoid offending the spirit within the stone.

- Totemism—a clan or group is represented by a particular animal; images (totems) of the animal are worshiped. Religious attention is focused on a few objects only. Critical scholars find an example of totemism in the making of a golden calf at Sinai (Exod 32:4; cf. 1

1. Armstrong, *History of God*, xx.

Kgs 12:28; Acts 7:41). Archaeological digs in Israel have unearthed a bronze bull in an ancient Israelite cultic site, dated from the period of the judges (c. 1200 BCE). This figurine, symbolizing power and fertility, apparently was associated with the worship of Yahweh (Israel's deity) as well as Baal (a deity of the neighboring Phoenicians).

- Polytheism—recognition of many higher powers, friendly and unfriendly. All are ranked higher than humans and have designated functions such as deities of war, love, agriculture, rain, and so forth. Polytheism is alleged to exist in the Pentateuch, where the chief title for God is Elohim, a term with a plural ending.

- Henotheism (also called "monolatry")—one god in a certain territory. This transition stage between polytheism and monotheism, based on the idea that each tribe, clan, or nation is ruled by a single god, suggests there are as many gods as there are nations or ethnic groups. This is alleged to be evident in the Israelite religion, which pitted the national god, Yahweh, against the gods of surrounding nations such as Baal and Astarte, deities of the Phoenicians (Judg 2:11–13), or Dagon, god of the Philistines (Judg 16:23).

- Monotheism—belief in the existence of only one God. According to Wellhausen, this stage was not consistently reached until the period of Israel's classical prophets.

What are we to make of the presence of religious evolution in the Bible? Was there a time when the Israelites were animists, totemists, or polytheists? Of course, given what we know about biological, social, and cultural evolution, and if we go back far enough, say to the Paleolithic (Old Stone) Age, everyone's ancestors were animists to some extent. That, however, is not the question we are asking. Rather, what we want to know is, does the Bible provide evidence that at some point in biblical history, say during the patriarchal period, the Israelites were animistic, totemistic, or polytheistic?

Admittedly there are references to such beliefs and practices in patriarchal times (otherwise how can one explain mention of "household gods" in Genesis 31:19–35?), but such references, including the examples given above about altars made out of unhewn stones, Jacob's stone pillow, and Abraham's residence by the oaks of Mamre, can be explained otherwise and need not be animistic. Nineteenth-century biblical scholars cautioned against applying an evolutionary straightjacket on cultural and religious history in general, including Israelite history. Some considered animistic references in the Bible to be holdovers from ancient times. However, before we fault Wellhausen for arguing that Israelite religion had developed in five stages, we must note that he also espoused Wilhelm Vatke's notion that Israelite religion had developed in three stages: the nature/fertility stage, the spiritual/ethical stage, and the priestly/legal stage.

We need to remember several things about Wellhausen's theory of evolutionary development, namely, that (1) according to the romantic ethos of the nineteenth century, which Wellhausen inherited, to label something as "primitive" is to hold it in esteem; and that (2) progress is not always one way or in a straight line. There is regress and decay. Wellhausen admired the passion of the eighth-century prophets but disparaged the legalism of the Deuteronomic Reform and the ritualism of the priestly writers. For Wellhausen, the religion of Israel ended in decay, preparing the way for the new religion of Christianity.

A helpful place to start our discussion of the theology of ancient Israel is 1 Kings 19, a passage that records a memorable experience of the prophet Elijah on Mount Sinai. Elijah (his name means "Yahweh is my God"), persecuted by Jezebel (King Ahab's Phoenician wife) for his faithfulness to Yahweh, has fled to Mount Sinai, where he prepares for an encounter with the divine: "Now there was a great wind, so strong that it was splitting mountains and breaking rocks in pieces before Yahweh, but Yahweh was not in the wind; and after the wind an earthquake, but Yahweh was not in the earthquake; and after the earthquake a fire, but Yahweh was not in the fire; and after the fire a sound of sheer silence" (1 Kgs 19:11–12; these last few words are traditionally translated "a still small voice").

This passage is often cited as a landmark in the history of Israelite religion, for it reveals an emerging distinction between polytheism and monotheism. In polytheism, the forces of nature may be inhabited by the gods, or loosely equated with them. But in the monotheism that was developing in Israel, there would be greater distance between nature and divinity.

Most Jews and Christians, whether observant or not, know that at the heart of the Torah lies the famous faith statement known as the Shema: "Hear O Israel: The Lord is our God, the Lord alone" (Deut 6:4). While that translation, taken from the NRSV, neither affirms nor denies monotheism (the Hebrew words can also be translated: "The Lord our God is one Lord," or "The Lord our God, the Lord is one," or "The Lord is our God, the Lord is one"), when Jews recite these words, they are clearly affirming monotheism. We cannot assume, however, that such was the original meaning.

The Roots of Christianity

In its biblical context, the statement "Hear O Israel" (Deut 5:1; 6:4) is proclaimed with great urgency. While Moses is said to be speaking at a time when the memory of the Exodus is still fresh and the people are faced with the hazards of entering Canaan, it is quite clear that the author has in mind another audience. Deuteronomy is primarily being addressed to a later generation, to "those who are not here with us today" (29:14-15). Biblical scholars tell us that the Shema—and its view of God—does not come from the eleventh century BCE (the Mosaic period) but rather from the seventh century BCE (the reign of Josiah and the time of the classical prophet Jeremiah), suggesting that monotheism, as we know it today, emerged relatively late in Israelite history.

The idea that other gods exist, but are not to be worshiped, is evident in the Ten Commandments. Understood as having been given by God, they represent the very heart of the law of the Jews. They begin with an interesting statement: "I am the Lord your God, who brought you out of the land of Egypt, out of the house of slavery; you shall have no other gods before me" (Exod 20:2). This text clearly presupposes the existence of other gods, but they are not to take precedence over the God of Israel. The text declares the God of Israel to be the only God for the Israelites, but it doesn't state that there are no other gods. Quite the contrary!

Eventually a strain of monotheism developed within ancient Israel, as is evident in Isaiah 45:5: "I am the Lord, and there is no other; besides me there is no god." However, this passage is dated to the sixth century BCE, long after Moses. Even as late as the time of Jesus, Jews who were monotheists also believed in divine beings such as angels and archangels, far more powerful than mortals. The basis for such beliefs is found in the Hebrew Bible, which mentions divine beings coming to earth as humans. Sometimes God also is said to appear on earth in human or some other form. Already in the book of Genesis Abraham is said to have an encounter with three "men"; later in the story, two are revealed to be angels and the third is God.

Another occurrence of an angel being identified as God occurs in Exodus 3, at the burning bush. Here Moses is addressed by the "angel of the Lord" (Exod 3:2), who is later identified as "the Lord" (Yahweh) and as God ("Elohim"). Other passages of the Bible tell us that angels can be called sons of God (see Job 1:6) or God himself, and that they become human. Perhaps the most famous instance of a "man" identified as God is the story of Jacob's

Christlikeness

wrestling match at Bethel in Genesis 32:24–30. Jacob's divine adversary had to vanish before sunrise, but not before giving Jacob a new name.

Viewing the doctrine of God as having changed through Israelite history contradicts what we were taught in church. Most of us never envisioned God as having evolved at all. We learned that God was there in the beginning, fully formed, that God gave form to everything else, and that the earliest humans, including Adam and Eve, the patriarchs, Moses, and Israel's religious leaders, were monotheists from the start. But that's not really the story in the Bible, at least not the whole story. "If you read the Hebrew Bible carefully, it tells the story of a god in evolution, a god whose character changes radically from beginning to end."[2]

The view that Israelite religion reached monotheism only after a period of henotheism (exclusive devotion to one god without denying the existence of others) is now widely accepted by biblical scholars, including by many practicing Jews and Christians, but things get more controversial when you suggest that there was a long time when Yahweh was ensconced in an Israelite pantheon, working alongside other gods. Let's examine the archaeological, biblical, and historical evidence, starting with the biblical account of the conquest of Canaan, to see if we can determine why a gap exists between scholars and rank-and-file Christians, most of whom believe monotheism was revealed to Moses, who then created a theocracy based on monotheistic faith.

According to the book of Joshua, the Canaanites, wicked polytheists, were conquered by monotheistic Israelites, led by Joshua: "Joshua defeated the whole land, the hill country and the Negeb and the lowland and the slopes, and all their kings; he left none remaining, but utterly destroyed all that breathed, as the Lord God of Israel commanded" (Josh 10:40). Religious conservatives rely on the findings of William Albright, sometimes called the founder of biblical archaeology, for support of this scenario. In his book *From the Stone Age to Christianity*, published in 1940, Albright affirmed that artifacts unearthed in Palestine (today's nation of Israel) paint a clear picture: Israelites had marched into Canaan from Egypt and swiftly destroyed and occupied Canaanite towns, rapidly replacing indigenous paganism with a radically different Yahwism. In his estimation, archaeological excavations showed an abrupt break between the Canaanite culture first encountered by the Israelites and the culture they built to replace it.

---

2. Wright, *Evolution of God*, 101.

Albright was a devout Christian, something that clearly impacted his findings. His views now lack foundation.

Recent decades of painstaking excavation and scientific archaeological research in the region supposedly conquered by the Israelites fail to provide evidence of a violent conquest by the Israelites. There isn't even much evidence to support a competing theory, that of a gradual, more peaceful influx of desert nomads gradually displacing Canaanites. While biblical archaeologists disagree about many things, there is now consensus that the Israelites who first settled in the highlands of Canaan were not foreign invaders but rather that they were Canaanites all along.

In the twelfth century BCE, as the Bronze Age was giving way to the Iron Age, there was political and economic disruption across the Middle East. Amid this chaos, new settlements, clearly Israelite, arose in Canaan. In all likelihood, the Israelites emerged from a particular line of Canaanites, a group which may have absorbed exiles from Egypt. One of these early Israelite settlements yielded an artifact that illustrates the cultural continuity between Israel and Canaan. The artifact is a small figurine of a bronze bull, exactly the kind of "Canaanite" idol that the Bible condemns.

In addition to figurines of Baal, recent archaeological digs in Israel have unearthed in ancient Israelite settings testimony of extensive devotion to Asherah, the Canaanite goddess of fertility and the wife of El. In the late twentieth century archaeologists discovered inscriptions, dating to around 800 BCE, at two different Israelite sites, one in the northern Sinai and another near Hebron in Judah. Both inscriptions invoke blessings "by Yahweh and his Asherah." In both cases the implication is that Asherah is a consort of Yahweh. The word "his" puts a suggestive spin, corroborated by a passage in 2 Kings 23:6, reporting that near the end of the seventh century (around 620 BCE), Asherah was worshiped in Yahweh's temple in Jerusalem.

As one would expect, there are numerous references to Asherah in the Bible, all disparaging. Her symbol was a sacred pole in a grove of trees near an altar (1 Kgs 16:33; 2 Kgs 21:3). The biblical writings regularly command destruction of these symbols (Deut 7:5; 12:3; 16:21). A crucial development in the evolution of monotheism occurred when a priest who didn't favor polytheism "brought out the image of Asherah from the house of the Lord, outside Jerusalem, to the Wadi Kidron, burned it at the Wadi Kidron, beat it to dust and threw the dust of it upon the graves of the common people" (2 Kgs 23:6). These passages attest to the pervasive polytheistic practices of the Israelites, late in the prophetic period; the fate of monotheism lay in the balance.

Such finds would not have surprised William Albright, for the Bible indicates that the Israelites occasionally worshiped idols. But the biblical story views such episodes as lapses in monotheism, a belief system brought to Canaan by Moses. However, few biblical scholars today agree with this assessment. They do not view biblical accounts of Moses to be historically reliable. Rather these stories are believed to have been recorded centuries after the events they describe, and then further redacted later by monotheists who wished to give their theology greater authority.

Increasingly it is suspected that an early pure Yahwism may never have existed except among a small minority of Yahweh devotees, or perhaps only in the minds of later revisionists such as the Deuteronomistic historians. The evidence seems to point to later Yahwism having emerged out of a greater Canaanite religion or out of a Yahwism indistinguishable from the Canaanite religion.

How Yahweh Became Yahweh[3]

From an objective standpoint, there is no reason to assume that the advent of Israelite monotheism took place anywhere other than Canaan, after centuries of immersion in Canaanite culture. It is also possible that Yahweh, who in the Bible expends so much effort denouncing Canaanite gods, actually started as a Canaanite deity.

Such a hypothesis is helpful because it addresses numerous problems in the biblical text, including (a) references to God speaking in the plural (see Gen 1:26–27; 3:22; 11:7. This use of the first-person plural by God, in both the P and J sources, seems to indicate that this language was originally part of the Israelites' tradition); (b) references to the "divine council" (Ps 82:1. Traditional explanations suggest that this reference is to angels, the heavenly host, or other supernatural beings, but Psalm 82:1 and 6 refer to "gods," and none of the above qualify as gods); and (c) the many titles for Yahweh in the Bible that include the word El:

- Elohim ("God"; "gods")
- El Elyon ("God Most High"; "Exalted One")

---

3. This segment is adapted from Wright, *Evolution of God*, 110–15.

- El Shaddai ("God Almighty"; "God of the Mountain")
- El Olam ("God of Eternity"; "The Everlasting God)
- El Roi ("God of Vision or Divining"; "God Who Sees")
- El Berith ("God of the Covenant")

Of these, the phrase El Shaddai is especially intriguing, for its meaning remains unclear; it seems to refer to mountains, not omnipotence. This name probably refers to El's localization in a mountainous region or to his theophany in mountain storms (cf. the "thunder and lightning" associated with the Sinai theophany, Exodus 19:16, and the "wind, earthquake, and fire in 1 Kings 19:11–12). In the time of the patriarchs the deity was identified with the storm god Hadad, often known as Baal among the Canaanites. After the patriarchal period, the original meaning of "Shaddai" was eclipsed, and the name occasionally was used as a synonym for "Yahweh." The author of Job favors this name, for it expressed the majesty and omnipotence of deity. The Septuagint renders "Shaddai" in the book of Job as Kurios ("Lord") or Pantocrator ("Almighty"), expressing aspects of God attractive to later Jews and Christians.

While El is the generic Semitic name for "God" or "deity," it was also the name for the Canaanite high god. "Given that the Canaanite El appears on the historical record before the Israelite god Yahweh, it is tempting to conclude that Yahweh in some way emerged from El, and may even have started life as a renamed version of El."[4] For instance, there are a few times in the Bible when the term El applied to Yahweh seems to be a proper noun. According to Genesis 33:20, Jacob "erected an altar and called it El-Elohe-Israel." This concept could be translated as "god, the god of Israel," but uncapitalized it wouldn't make much sense. Some English translations of Genesis render the expression as "El, God of Israel." Perhaps an even closer link between Israelite religion and El can be found in the word "Israel," which ends in "el" and means "El does battle," "El contends," or "El perseveres." In ancient times names were often inspired by gods, and names ending in "el" typically referred to the god El.

For present purposes, of interest is the way "El Shaddai" is used in Exodus 6:3, in a conversation between Moses and God. God says: "I am Yahweh. I appeared to Abraham, to Isaac, and to Jacob as El Shaddai, but

---

4. Wright, *Evolution of God*, 111.

by my name Yahweh I did not make myself known to them." Here even Yahweh claims to have started life in Canaan with the name El.

If you were crafting a history of your god, would you add such an odd twist, saying that he used to go by another name? Wouldn't such an oddity fit better if one were trying to convince two religious groups—one worshiping a god called Yahweh and another a god called El—that they actually worship the same god? This is precisely the suggestion of the Documentary Hypothesis, that at some point in Israelite history there were two geographically distinct traditions to reconcile, one worshiping a god named El (the E author lived in the north, closer to the heartland of El worship) and one worshiping a god named Yahweh (the J author lived in the south, in part of Israel known as Judah).

Certainly the Bible holds hints of once separate groups having united. It describes Israel at the end of the second millennium BCE, before it evolved into a monarchical state, as a confederation of twelve tribes. The merging of Israel's tribes is also reflected in the patriarchal story: Abraham begat Isaac, who begat Jacob. Few scholars consider this lineage accurate, but most think it significant.

The idea that Israel coalesced near or in the region of El worship and only adopted Yahweh later, while absorbing tribes from the south, gains support from the famous Merneptah Stele, an ancient Egyptian stone inscription from 1219 BCE, on which the name "Israel" first appears historically. The word clearly refers to a people, not a place, but the people seem to have been Canaanites. The stele does not mention Yahweh; its only possible allusion to any god is the "el" in Israel. And centuries would pass before a text would mention both Israel and "Yhwh" (the ancient spelling of Yahweh, before Semitic languages were written with vowels). Intriguingly, there are separate Egyptian references to "Yhw" even earlier than that first reference to Israel, but here "Yhw" seems to be a place, not a god. And that place "seems to have been somewhere around Edom, in southern Canaan, which makes sense if a Yahweh-worshiping people from the south eventually merged with an El-worshiping people to the north."[5] As the name Israel indicates, over time a group of Israelites transformed the concept "El the warrior" to Yahweh the warrior, styling itself nationally after this deity. At first Yahweh came to be regarded as Israel's God and only long afterwards as the God of the universe.

---

5. Wright, *Evolution of God*, 114.

Most of us grew up hearing stories about Elijah, a classic Israelite prophet who defended monotheism without compromise in his conflict with Jezebel and the prophets of Baal, but even this great hero cannot be considered a monotheist, since he advocated monolatry rather than true monotheism. He didn't necessarily deny Baal's existence (the monotheistic position), just that Baal was not worthy of Israelite worship. The first "effective monotheist" seems to have been the prophet Amos, although later classical prophets developed his ideas further. It took an event and a person to develop monotheistic belief most thoroughly, an event known as the Babylonian Exile and an unknown prophet called Second Isaiah. It was this event, called "the furnace of adversity" (Isa 48:10), that led to the monotheistic standard the masses would accept.

Two themes catapulted Second Isaiah to popularity, first within Judaism and later in Christianity. The first theme is that God alone is the God of the whole earth: "I am the Lord, and there is no other; beside me there is no god" (Isa 45:5); "I am the Lord, who made all things, who alone stretched out the heavens, who by myself spread out the earth" (Isa 44:24). Biblical scholars cite Second Isaiah as a landmark, and deservedly so. Finally, after centuries of monolatry, monotheistic declarations come with clarity and force. The second theme, that God will "bring forth justice to the nations," gets as much attention as monotheism. What kind of God is this God? What is God's stance toward the world? The answer is inspiring: God is universal not only in power but also in concern, and this gives God's people a momentous mission: "I will give you as a light to the nations, that my salvation may reach to the end of the earth" (Isa 49:6).

Conclusion

While the cult of Yahweh is the principal concern of the Old Testament, it may not have been the primary religious concern of the Israelites. The common masses participated in syncretistic beliefs and practices throughout the pre-exilic period, while a small minority were monolatrists, belonging to what scholars call the "Yahweh alone" movement. This minority wrote the biblical texts and projected their beliefs into the distant past to give the impression their monotheism was the norm from which Israelites deviated.

In the early 1970s Morton Smith became the first biblical scholar to propose seriously that the Yahwism-alone movement was a minority religio-political movement in the pre-exilic period, in opposition to the royal cult and all popular or familial forms of religion. Smith traced the movement's development through five stages:

1. During the pre-monarchic and monarchic periods, Israel shared the common religious perspective of the ancient Near East. Each region had a national deity and Yahweh was the national god of Israel. Properly speaking, Yahweh was the deity of the dynastic rulers in Judah and Israel. His status was like that of Chemosh in Moab or Milcom in Ammon. Perhaps a few elements within Israel had a proclivity to worship one universal god, but their impact was minimal.
2. From the time of David (1000 BCE), the court of Judah may have been responsible for popularizing the worship of Yahweh among the masses.
3. In the northern nation of Israel, a move toward monotheism began with the Omride conflict (850–840), when Jezebel persecuted and killed Yahwistic prophets. However, the overthrow of the Omrides (kings Omri and Ahab) resulted from their foreign connections rather than from a desire to elevate Yahweh monotheistically.
4. Classical prophets and the Deuteronomic Reform movement brought the message of practical monotheism to the masses. Amos and Hosea were forerunners among the prophets in 750 BCE. Despite attempts at reform (probably more political than religious) by kings Hezekiah (c. 700 BCE) and Josiah (621 BCE), by 580 BCE monotheism appears to have been in the minority once again.
5. In the exilic and post-exilic eras the people became monotheists, for by then people living under foreign rule and influence had to make a clear decision about participating in those cults. Restraint in the fact of such pressure makes people true monotheists.

The constant biblical rhetoric against syncretism and idolatry should not be seen as evidence of monotheism, but rather as admission that pure Yahwism was in the minority. During the pre-exilic period most Israelites were polytheists, worshiping Yahweh along other gods, and they saw this as perfectly acceptable. Initially, the elevation of Yahweh for exclusive veneration was an act of nationalistic expression, as one might find in a time of crisis. Ultimately, in the post-exilic era, priestly laws separated the Jews from others and encouraged pure monotheism.

The Roots of Christianity

Questions for Discussion and Reflection

Select one or more of the following questions and write your answer(s) in a journal. If you are in a group study, be prepared to share your answers with those in the group.

1. Assess the merit of Bertrand Russell's concept of "parochialism in time." In as strong a way as possible, make a persuasive case for our connectedness to the past and for every person's need to study not only Western history but world history.

2. When you worship, which God do you worship? The God of Moses or of Jesus? The God of Aquinas or of Luther? The God of Martha or of Mary? The God of Jonathan Edwards or of Martin Luther King? Explain your answer.

3. Assess the merits of the notion that Israelite religion evolved through distinct stages in its understanding of God. Can we square this concept with the popular notion among conservative Jews and Christians that ancestors of their faith such as Abraham and Moses were monotheists, having ideas of God received through divine revelation rather than through a human process of understanding and discovery? Explain your answer.

4. Assess the merits of the statement, "If you read the Hebrew Bible carefully, it tells the story of a god in evolution, a god whose character changes radically form beginning to end."

5. In your estimation, do the Ten Commandments reflect the perspective known as henotheism or that of monotheism? Explain your answer.

6. If you were to accept the conclusions of most biblical scholars that the Israelites were Canaanites in origin rather than foreign invaders, would this change your views of biblical authority? Explain your answer.

7. Assess the merits of the notion that the various biblical names and titles for God reflect polytheistic rather than monotheistic understandings of God.

8. Were the first Israelites pagan? Explain your answer.

5

Jewish Wisdom Spirituality

ABOUT ONE THIRD OF the Hebrew Bible is poetry. Awareness of this feature of Israel's liturgical and literary expression is invaluable for reading and interpreting scripture. Poetry is a personal way of expressing faith, both individually and communally. Poetry appeals to our human nature, making us realize the importance of emotion and signifying that we are more than intellect.

While Israel's poetic literature was adaptable to both private devotion and corporate worship, Israel's wisdom spirituality focused on the individual. Through stirring teachings, the sages of the biblical wisdom tradition offer time-honored advice about some of life's most difficult questions, including the problem of pain, the suffering of the innocent, the nature of evil, the justice of God, and dealing with death. They also address such themes as friendship, virtue and vice, marriage and spousal choice, decision-making, life priorities, child rearing, illness, and death. The insights offered in the biblical tradition and the efforts of the biblical sages to integrate faith, reason, revelation, and human wisdom rival those of the renowned philosophical schools of ancient Greece.

In Israel there were probably three separate settings for wisdom teaching: the clan, the court of the king, and the school. In the clan, the father and mother were the sages. In the royal court, the kings were associated with sages who advised them (see 2 Sam 16:23; 17:14). Later wisdom writings give evidence of a house of learning, that is, a school in which sages instructed the young. The primary purpose of the book of Proverbs is to instruct youth in the life of wisdom, principally the children of wealthy elite connected to the royal court. It is likely that Ecclesiastes also emerged from school instruction, its author a scribe or teacher who lived in Jerusalem. The reference to "those who are wise" in Daniel 12:3 points to a group of trained scholars who served as exemplars in society, praised and viewed in tandem with "those who lead many to righteousness."

Biblical wisdom literature includes not only Proverbs, Job, and Ecclesiastes, but the deuterocanonical books of Sirach and the Wisdom of Solomon. While these books have provided perspective, guidance, and consolation to generations of believers, they can also be of significance for unbelievers, precisely because this literature provides perspective to some of humanity's greatest concerns, including suffering, educating our young, governing wisely, avoiding temptation and vice, growing in virtue, choosing better vocations, selecting friends, and choosing marriage partners.

While the Torah and the prophets agreed in placing the nation at the center, during the period of the Restoration, the individual gradually came to the fore. Personal happiness and success, together with individual fears and hopes, had been recognized in the Torah and by the prophets, but after the exile, the problem of individual suffering became central to Jewish thought. Increasingly, too, the prophets, concerned with the ideal future of the nation, focused on the happiness of the individual. "It was the decline of faith in the fortunes of the nation, coupled with the growth of interest in the individual and with individual destiny, that stimulated the development of wisdom. Wisdom was not concerned with the group, but with the individual, with the realistic present rather than with a longed-for future."[1]

In ancient Israel there were three principal intellectual and spiritual currents, found in the three sections of the Hebrew Bible: Torah (the Law), Nebiim (the Prophets), and Ketubim (the Writings). The Septuagint, the Greek version of the Hebrew scriptures, expanded the Writings to include a fourth category: Wisdom Literature, adding to that literature the books of Sirach and the Wisdom of Solomon. A tripartite division of scripture appears in Sirach: "How different the one who devotes himself to the study of the law of the Most High! He seeks out the wisdom of all the ancients and is concerned with prophecies" (38:34b–39:1). What is unusual about this division is that "wisdom" is placed second, after "law" but before "prophecy." The passage extols the activity of the scribe as one who preserves the sayings of the famous and penetrates the subtleties of parables; he seeks

---

1. Gordis, *God and Man*, 40.

out the hidden meanings of proverbs and is at home with the obscurities of parables" (34:2–3).

It is clear that Hebrew wisdom was not an isolated creation in Israel. On the contrary, it was part of a vast intellectual activity that had been cultivated for centuries in the Fertile Crescent, especially in Egypt and Babylonia. Situated at the cultural crossroads of the ancient world, the Israelites were influenced from an early time by Eastern wisdom writings. These writings, which circulated far beyond the land of their origin, dated back to the Egyptian Pyramid Age (about 2600–2175 BCE) and to the Sumerian era in Mesopotamia. However, wisdom had a timeless quality, transcending time and culture. Though ancient sages reflected on problems of society as they knew them, these were human problems found in varying forms in every society. Thus the wisdom movement was fundamentally international.

According to the historian Charles A. Beard, one of the lessons of history can be summarized by the proverb, "The bee fertilizes the flower it robs."[2] This is particularly true of the Jews during the exile and the Restoration. Although the experience seemed bitter to many at the time, the people came to realize that God was working for good. While the surrounding culture was regarded as a threat to Israel's faith, the exile also awakened a new world-consciousness, enlarging Israel's faith to an extent never before seen, not even in the cosmopolitan age of Solomon. The exiles realized that they must look beyond their own community to the whole civilized world, if they would behold the glory and majesty of God's purpose in history. The time was ripe for a deeper understanding of the conviction that Israel was called to be God's agent in bringing blessings to all the nations of the earth.

The view that world-shaking events may have a double and seemingly contradictory effect on people's lives characterized a small but highly literate and influential group of Palestinian Jews living in Judah under Persian rule during the fourth and fifth centuries BCE. These sages flourished during this "Golden Age of Wisdom," a peaceful era of two hundred years aided by a common lingua franca (Aramaic) across the Persian empire, a new sense of Jewish identity, and a new internationalism. During this period the books of Job and Ecclesiastes were written and the wisdom material found in the book of Proverbs was collected and finalized.

The wisdom of the biblical sages, unlike the regulations of the priests or the oracles of the prophets, usually made no claim to being divine revelation. It was, of course, self-evident that God was the source of Hebrew

---

2. Cited in Anderson, *Understanding the Old Testament*, 425.

Jewish Wisdom Spirituality

wisdom, as of every creative aspect of human nature. Thus, when Isaiah described the ideal Davidic king who would govern in justice and wisdom, he envisioned the spirit of the Lord resting upon him, "the spirit of wisdom and understanding, the spirit of counsel and might, the spirit of knowledge and the fear of the Lord" (Isa 11:2). Some of wisdom's most fervent advocates went further. By endowing wisdom with a cosmic role, they sought to win for wisdom a status almost equal to that of Torah and prophecy. In their most lavish praise of wisdom, the Hebrew sages attributed her with great antiquity, declaring her to have been established "at the first, before the beginning of the earth" (Prov 8:23). In Job's magnificent "Hymn to Wisdom" (Job 28), wisdom is endowed with cosmic significance and is virtually personified (28:20-28).

In Palestinian Judaism, where the study and interpretation of the Torah ultimately produced the Mishnah, wisdom was equated with the Mosaic law. In the Diaspora, outside of Palestine, where Greek ideas were more influential, wisdom received a more philosophic interpretation. In the case of Philo, the celebrated Alexandrian Jew of the first-century CE, wisdom assumed the doctrine of the Logos or the Divine Word, which became the instrument by which God creates and governs the universe. It is only a further step to conceive of the Divine Word as the intermediary between God and the world, even as a distinct "person" or "aspect" of the divine nature (cf. the Logos Hymn in John 1:1-5).

Ultimately, however, biblical wisdom's claim to authority rested on its pragmatic truth. The Hebrew sages insisted that the application of wisdom "worked," meaning that when coupled with human reason and careful observation, it brought human beings success and happiness. Its origin might be in heaven, but its justification was to be sought in society and nature: "keep sound wisdom and prudence, and they will be life for your soul and adornment for your neck. Then you will walk on your way securely and your foot will not stumble. If you sit down, you will not be afraid; when you lie down, your sleep will be sweet. Do not be afraid of sudden panic, or of the storm that strikes the wicked; for the Lord will be your confidence and will keep your foot from being caught" (Prov 3:19-26).

The Underlying Principle for Israel's Sages

What was the goal of Israel's sages? What did they hope to achieve by coining proverbs and formulating observations about the meaning of life? One means of discovering the self-consciousness of Israel's sages as a distinct group within society is to examine the carefully worded introduction to the book of Proverbs, where we find listed a cluster of words and phrases that characterize those who master the proverbial tradition: wisdom, instruction, understanding, intelligence, righteousness, justice, equity, discretion, knowledge, prudence, learning, and skill. Taken together, they constitute individual facets of the quest for "Life," what philosophers call "the good life." The canonical sages pursued the good life in all its manifestations: health, wealth, honor, progeny, longevity, and remembrance.

A study of four books central to the Jewish wisdom spirituality reveals different results in describing the object of the sapiential search:[3]

1. The book of Proverbs represents a quest for *practical knowledge*, an understanding about nature and human beings that enable people to live wisely and well. For the authors of Proverbs, finding "life" means not so much biologically but relationally, life with another. For the sage, "to live" means to live with wisdom, to banquet with her in her house. According to Proverbs 9:4, living with wisdom is the opposite of living in ignorance. To live with wisdom requires "pondering," meaning that one must live with discernment. Living with the proverbs is like living in a house or a school of wisdom, where wise sayings are examined deeply. Hence the proverbial material is often couched in parables, allegories, riddles, and other enigmatic sayings, with emphasis on subtlety, paradox, and wordplay. Proverbial themes may appear simplistic or repetitive, but careful study reveals that details are important and vital to the meaning of the text.

2. The book of Job is not primarily a search for knowledge about how to cope with the enigmas of ordinary existence, but rather represents a quest for *God's presence*. The author, like the character of Job, acknowledges God's gracious presence in the past, and therefore cannot endure a God who is hidden in the present. Job searches the darkest depths of despair in pursuit of his God, and eventually risks death and even damnation to achieve restored communion. To Job, God is "Life," the highest good, and compared to that *summum bonum*, biological life pales.

3. The book of Ecclesiastes represents the quest for *meaning in a silent universe*. Like Job, Qoheleth (the author of Ecclesiastes) cannot affirm

3. The following analysis is adapted from Crenshaw, *Old Testament Wisdom*, 62–65.

Jewish Wisdom Spirituality

biological life as the supreme good, but unlike Job, Qoheleth does not enter into dialogue with the living God. Lacking confidence in life's goodness, he searches in vain for some meaning that can enable him to endure his empty existence.

4. The book of Sirach represents the quest for Jewish *identity and continuity* in a Hellenistic world that esteemed quite different cultural and religious values. His intention is to convince Jewish youth that Greeks are not the only ones with a magnificent intellectual heritage. Highlighting the role of tradition for oneself and for one's community, his goal is tantamount to survival of the Jewish religion and way of life.

Each book, in addition to representing a different object of search, also provides a different temporal focus. The book of Proverbs looks to the distant past, when God established a pattern for the cosmos and for life. The book of Job, focusing on suffering, is concerned wholly with the present. Qoheleth is unable to discern any future worth living for, since death is the great leveler and silencer of hope. Sirach looks to Israel's glorious past in order to provide his generation the ability to resist cultural compromise in the present and thereby give a future to Diaspora Jews. Invariably, Israel's sages, whatever their goals, arrive at a closed door called Mystery, and none except God hold the key to this room. This understanding is what Proverbs 25:2 affirms when it declares that God's glory lies in the tendency to conceal essential reality.

There is a fundamental paradox in the Jewish sapiential tradition, for wisdom is both an object of search but also a gift from God. A relentless search oscillates between two extremes, trusting in one's ability to secure existence and dependence upon God's mercy. The latter, however, represents the final word, for the ultimate quest is that of a gracious God in search of humanity. For humans, the bottom line seems clear: self-discipline, coupled with trust, leads to joy: "When you get hold of [wisdom], do not let her go. For at last you will find the rest she gives, and she will be changed into joy for you" (Sir 6:27–28).

In one sense wisdom authors are highly conservative, for they revere tradition. Yet in another sense they are highly innovative and progressive, for they also revere their own experience and value their own insights. In the biblical tradition, the understanding and insight that constitute "wisdom" ultimately come from God, but are accessible in three primary forms: wisdom taught by God, wisdom taught by nature, and wisdom that arises from reflection on human experience. In these writings, wisdom is the rare attainment of intelligence, sound judgment, ethical conduct, humility, and the distinctive piety identified in the motto of the book of Proverbs: "The fear of the Lord is the beginning of wisdom" (Prov 9:10). Within the biblical wisdom tradition, certain themes take on increasing significance: the fear of the Lord, God's self-manifestation through personified wisdom, the problem of innocent suffering, the meaning of life, the justification of God's ways, the limits of human knowledge, and the inevitability of death. Given the range of this literature, we may conclude that Israel's sages struggled with life's fundamental questions. Their way of addressing these, and the solutions they reached, point to a remarkable group of people.

Wisdom's practical goals for temporal success appealed primarily to those groups in society that benefitted from the status quo—government officials, rich merchants, great landowners, even high-priestly families. The goal of upper-class education was the training of youth for successful careers. These needs were admirably met by the wisdom teachers who arose, primarily in Jerusalem, the capital city.

The upper-class orientation reflected in the book of Job emerges in the treatment of the book's basic theme—the problem of suffering. While wisdom writers could not ignore the inequities of the present order. at the same time, as representatives of affluent social groups, they did not find the status quo intolerable. The lower classes, oppressed by poverty and marginalized at the hands of domestic and foreign masters, were deeply afflicted by the prosperity of the wicked and the suffering of the righteous. Holding resolutely to their faith in God, they were nevertheless unable to see divine justice operating in the world. Their solution to this problem was the espousal of the doctrine of the afterlife, a future world where the inequalities of the present order would be rectified. Thus, the idea of life after death became an integral feature of Pharisaic Judaism and of Christianity.

Jewish wisdom spirituality profoundly influenced the New Testament community. Wisdom images and ideas appear in every layer of the New Testament, from the letter of James, an early document attributed to the brother of Jesus, to the gospels, which portray Jesus as a wisdom teacher, to the letters of Paul, where Christ is called the wisdom of God (1 Cor 1:24). Early christological hymns, embedded in the New Testament, utilize wisdom motifs to express Christian belief in the incarnation of Jesus (John 1:1–18) and in his cosmic rule (Col 1:15–20; Heb 1:1–4). Among the various influences on the New Testament was the identification of wisdom

Jewish Wisdom Spirituality

(Jesus) with divine spirit (2 Cor 3:16–18), word (John 1:1), and law (Matt 5:17–20; 7:24–29). The study of Jewish wisdom literature as found in the Hebrew Bible provides readers of the New Testament with an entirely new and intriguing perspective on Jesus and early Christianity. Following the resurrection of Jesus, when early Christians were looking for language and concepts to express their experience and understanding of Jesus, one of the most helpful resources was the wisdom literature. Of course, other parts of the Hebrew Bible were valuable, such as the prophets, the psalms, and the historical traditions of Israel, but the authors of the New Testament and the leaders of the early Christian communities found in wisdom spirituality an important resource for understanding Jesus and their new life in Christ.

Wisdom and Spirituality

A strong correlation can be found between the wisdom tradition and spirituality, particularly if spirituality represents the ability to live life authentically, for wisdom thinkers found ordinary human existence fascinating. Kathleen O'Connor, a Roman Catholic religious educator, views wisdom as a form of spirituality for the market place. Such spirituality represents the arena "where humans struggle to cope with the chaos of daily life, where Wisdom and Folly compete for human loyalties, and where the divine and the human meet."[4] A spirituality for the market place points equally to two aspects of the natural world; (a) a realm or sphere of life wherein humans might expect to meet God, and (b) a way of living in the world. Popular thinking often limits divine-human exchange to specifically religious activities and places, claiming that God is to be found primarily in the privacy of the individual soul. Wisdom literature provides a resource for a more holistic spirituality, one that perceives outer and inner life, individual and community life, and God and the world as inextricably intertwined. Understanding the realm of divine-human encounter to be ordinary human life, wisdom promotes the pathway of relationship.

The implications for such an understanding of spirituality are enormous. Wisdom spirituality leaves little room for dualistic thinking or living. Ordinary life and the life of faith are not separate or antithetical spheres, for all life exists in the presence of its Creator. From wisdom's perspective, the struggles and conflicts of daily life should not to be shunned or avoided as though they are evil, but rather embraced in full consciousness of their

4. O'Connor, *Wisdom Literature*, 14.

revelatory and healing potential. When Israel's wisdom literature focuses on mundane concerns, it is not ignoring but assuming faith.

Wisdom's focus on human concerns has caused some biblical interpreters to question the presence of this literature in the Bible, but these books should not be viewed as secular orphans next to their more theological siblings, the law, the prophets, the gospels, or the epistles. In defending wisdom's viewpoint by referring to it as "theological anthropology," Roland Murphy makes the point that by starting with the realm of human experience, wisdom writers were not excluding God from their world, but rather focusing on what it means to be human in the presence of God. Murphy maintains that the modern distinction between the realms of the secular and the sacred never existed in Israel. Wisdom does not impose God on life but assumes God's presence and activity in every facet of its existence. The various wisdom books all agree that to be wise is to live harmoniously with one's community, the earth, and the creator.

Wisdom literature appreciates the ambiguity of human experience. It finds in ambiguity and confusion the opportunity for breakthrough into mystery. It struggles against rote religious answers to human problems. According to wisdom, life is not a simple set of truths to be followed indiscriminately, but a continual encounter with conflicting truths, each making competing claims upon the seeker. The subject matter of Proverbs, Job, Ecclesiastes, and the Song of Solomon is profoundly ambiguous and paradoxical. Opposing truths are set side by side and in some instances left unresolved. This is evident in the basic literary genre of wisdom, the *mashal*, a pithy saying, proverb, or riddle (see Prov 30:4, a riddle whose answer seems to be "God"; cf. Job 38:5–11). For the sages, life itself is a *mashal*, a world of ambiguity, a series of puzzles small and great. However, the point of ambiguity or paradox is not to bring the individual to an intellectual impasse or a spiritual angst, but to lead one beyond the obvious into deeper understanding. Offering a spirituality of discovery, wisdom requires openness, discernment, and choice. Because wisdom views life as paradoxical, it also calls for patience, trust, and a glad heart.

According to Israel's sages, humans live in a moral universe. Discovering this "rational rule" enabled the sages to protect their existence by acting in harmony with the fundamental order that sustains the cosmos. One's conduct either strengthens the existing order or contributes to the forces of chaos that threaten survival itself. Once the sages discovered this moral or rational principle, it became their task to transfer it from the realm of nature to the human sphere. They accomplished this goal through analogy. Close observation of nature and the animal kingdom convinced Israel's sages that the world was truly a harmonious entity (see Prov 30:19). The search for proper analogies had as its goal the securing of life. Those who successfully achieved correct knowledge purchased longevity for themselves, together with other indications of divine favor. Knowledge was therefore a means to an end, never an end itself.

While Israel's wisdom literature stands by itself in the Jewish corpus, from a very early period the wisdom movement exerted a pervasive influence on Israel's historical, prophetic, and poetic literature. Certain passages in Isaiah (9:6; 11:2, 9; 28:23–29; 31:2) emphasize wisdom and understanding, so much so that some scholars consider Isaiah to have been a sage before he became a prophet. Similar conclusions have been reached concerning Amos, whose home town of Tekoa is said to have been a center of wisdom. By way of support, scholars point to his universalistic message (whereby all nations are subjected to God's judgment), his use of special vocabulary such as the word "right," his use of unusual rhetorical devices (such as the "woe" sayings), and linguistic phenomena such as numerical sayings, all of which place Amos squarely within clan wisdom. Similar arguments have led to the claim that Micah and Jonah wrote under the influence of the wisdom tradition. Within the historical literature, the Succession Narrative (2 Samuel 9–20 and 1 Kings 1–2) has been attributed to a wisdom writer who sought to illustrate the teachings of certain parables (see Nathan's rebuke of David in 2 Samuel 12) into his narrative, telling stories that embody eternal truths. The same goes for the Joseph Narrative in Genesis, which may have been written by a sage in the royal court to serve as a model for professional courtiers. The association of court stories and wisdom in the book of Esther has led some interpreters to conclude that the author was a sage who wished to emphasize the rewards that come to those who combine wisdom with integrity. The primeval history in Genesis 1–11 has been found to exhibit wisdom influence, particularly in references to a tree of knowledge and to the concept of the knowledge of good and evil. The entire book of Deuteronomy, which emphasizes retribution, life and death (see 30:15–20), and the importance of observing God's commandments, has been attributed to sapiential authorship. Some scholars argue that wisdom gave birth to apocalyptic, pointing to Daniel's association with the legacy of the sages, both Babylonian (1:4) and Israelite (12:3). Eventually, Israel's wisdom literature was fully integrated into Israel's historical faith, as evidenced by the identification of Torah and wisdom in a group of "wisdom psalms" and by the combining of familiar personalities and the events of Israel's history with the wisdom tradition in the later books of Sirach and the Wisdom of Solomon.

Although most people today do not turn to the wisdom literature for prophetic inspiration, the wisdom method of reflection on life experience is gaining prominence. People are again recognizing that God is encountered *through* human experience, not despite it. In their quest for wisdom, students of biblical wisdom literature will be encouraged to know that sacred learning—including study and intellectual questioning—is and always has been at the heart of true spirituality. Those who read this literature will be exposed to a set of core values necessary for vital citizenship and effective leadership at all levels of life. They will also obtain time-honored advice about how to deal with life's uncertainties in a holistic and pragmatic manner, because biblical wisdom is based upon theological tenets such as monotheism, God's providential care for humanity, the moral nature of the universe, and the notion of covenant. Such tenets promote the perspective that people who belong to communities of faith are related to God in patterns of worship, trust, love, obedience, service, protection, and grace.

Questions for Discussion and Reflection

Select one or more of the following questions and write your answer(s) in a journal. If you are in a group study, be prepared to share your answers with those in the group.

1. If one third of the Hebrew Bible is poetic and one third of the gospel material is parabolic, what does this say about the role, purpose, and interpretation of scripture?
2. Explain and assess the implications of the author's statement that "The insights offered in the biblical tradition and the efforts of the biblical sages to integrate faith, reason, revelation, and human wisdom rival those of the renowned philosophical schools of ancient Greece."
3. In your estimation, what does wisdom literature teach us about the role of community in spirituality?
4. In your estimation, what does wisdom literature teach us about private and individual spirituality?

Jewish Wisdom Spirituality

5. Of Israel's three canonical books of wisdom (Proverbs, Job, Ecclesiastes), which do you find most relevant to your life today? Explain your answer.

6. In your estimation, after reading this chapter, what is the primary insight you gained from Charles Beard's statement that "one of the lessons of history can be summarized by the proverb, 'The bee fertilizes the flower it robs.'"

7. In your estimation, after reading this chapter, what is the primary insight you gained from the biblical sages about the place of wisdom in spirituality?

8. In your estimation, how did Jewish wisdom spirituality influence the early Christian understanding the person and message of Jesus?

9. In your estimation, what is the primary insight you gained from the segment "Wisdom and Spirituality." Explain your answer.

6

The Greco-Roman Roots of Christianity

WHAT WE CALL WESTERN civilization is a project that grew from a synthesis between Greek philosophical tradition and the Roman political, economic, and military tradition. Likewise, what we call Christianity is a project that grew from a synthesis between Jewish apocalyptic and wisdom tradition and cultural influences from Platonism, Stoicism, and other philosophical groups prevalent in the Greco-Roman environment. Much as Christianity could not have emerged apart from Judaism, it could not have developed apart from Ebionitism, gnosticism, Valentinianism, Marcionism, and other movements later labeled "heretical" or non-orthodox.[1] In this regard, neither would Augustine have developed his thought apart from Manicheism and Neoplatonism, Aquinas apart from Augustine, Protestantism apart from Catholicism, Liberal theology apart from orthodox theology, and Neo-orthodoxy apart from Liberalism.

As we saw in chapters 4 and 5 above, Christianity began as a sect within Judaism. Unlike other religions, including Judaism, Christianity was, from the outset, a religion that emphasized belief. It stressed that Jews, along with all other unbelievers, needed to believe that Jesus was the Messiah, God's long-awaited redeemer who would save believers from their sins. We see this belief in Jesus as Redeemer already in the earliest Christian sources, the letters of Paul, written between twenty to thirty years after Jesus' death, well before the appearance of the first gospels. In his letters, Paul indicates

---

1. For further discussion of these movements, see my chapter "Early Christianities" in *Response to the Other*, 128–44.

that Jesus is the fulfillment of the written scriptures of the Jews. For Paul, belief in Jesus is essential, the only way to be right with God.

From the beginning, then, Christianity was structured as a religion that de-emphasized cultic acts such as sacrifice and emphasized proper belief. Christians did not perform sacrifices to their God because they believed Jesus was the perfect and complete sacrifice. Their religion was based on accepting the sacrifice of Jesus on their behalf, rather than on performing sacrifices on his behalf. In this respect, Christianity was a religion of belief rather than of cultic act.

Moreover, unlike other religions of the Greek and Roman period, Christianity was exclusivistic. No other religion—perhaps excepting Judaism, although, as we have seen, ancient Judaism was not as exclusivistic as we might think—insisted that to worship their god, you could not worship other gods. Ancient religions were inclusivistic, accepting one another. If someone decided to worship a new god, such as when one moved to a new town and wished to adopt its deity, that didn't require giving up one's former god or gods. Many gods were believed to exist, all desiring worship. Christianity, however, claimed that the only way to be right with God was through belief in Jesus. This teaching made other religions wrong, and Christianity right. Faith or belief in Jesus made Christianity unique in the ancient world, its missionary consciousness contributing to its expansion and widespread growth.

This emphasis on belief also brought Christianity into contact with pagan philosophical schools prevalent in Greco-Roman culture. Many educated Christians, together with certain Hellenized Jews, engaged philosophically with their pagan counterparts, intellectualizing and mythologizing their belief system to make it more accessible, attractive, and compatible with philosophical tradition. The emphasis on exclusivism, however, exaggerated the need for proto-orthodox Christians to be correct in what they believed, adhering more literally to the developing apostolic tradition, refining what it meant to believe in Jesus. As a result, they felt they had to be precise about Jesus, who he was and what he taught, and what Christians needed to believe if they were to be right with God. If salvation depended upon belief, Christianity needed to clarify what had to be believed. As it turned out, different opinions emerged as to who Jesus was and what it meant to believe in him. Different theologies, christologies, and soteriologies developed and came to be embraced. Controversies ensued and soon creeds came into being, different Christian groups affirming different beliefs.

Each group needed its own authority for what it believed, and each claimed that its beliefs were rooted in the teachings of Jesus' apostles and, through them, to Jesus himself. In particular, each group stressed that its authority was based on its own sacred writings, allegedly produced by one or more apostles of Jesus. Distinct groups emerged, favoring certain writings over others.

The Role of Philosophy in Antiquity

Among the Greeks and Romans of the classical age, philosophy occupied the place taken by religion in our time. Unlike Sophists, who taught pupils techniques of persuasion, most philosophers, following Socrates, provided their pupils with a philosophy of life: they taught them what things in life were worth pursuing and how best to pursue them. Some of the parents who wanted a philosophical education for their child hired a philosopher to act as live-in tutor. Others would have sent their sons—but probably not their daughters—to a school of philosophy.

In antiquity, philosophy was the deeper religion of most intelligent people. Its concepts provided thinkers—pagan, Jewish, and Christian—with an intellectual framework for expressing their ideas. At the beginning of the Hellenistic period we find six main schools—Platonism, Aristotelianism, Pythagoreanism, Cynicism, Epicureanism, and Stoicism, of which those of Plato and Aristotle soon lost ground, although the former in the Neoplatonism of Plotinus later became once again prominent. On the border between philosophy and religion was Pythagoreanism. Pythagoras of Samos (c. 570–c. 490 BCE) paid great attention to numbers. He gathered about himself a group of followers to whom he communicated secret symbols and metaphysical lore, including belief in the transmigration of souls. Members of the Pythagorean brotherhood were vegetarians and viewed the body as the seat of all impure passions. Ultimately, certain aspects of Pythagoreanism were adopted by various gnostic systems of the early Christian period. Though nosticism took many different forms, a characteristic teaching of all gnostics was the fundamental antithesis between the material and the spiritual universe. Only the spiritual element in humans could receive redemption, gained through a secret knowledge or *gnosis* concerning knowledge of God and of the origin and destiny of all living beings.

Pythagoreanism and Platonism (known as Middle Platonism) enjoyed a revival from the first century BCE, but the three schools that held the stage were the Cynic, Epicurean, and Stoic. The aim of all three may be summed up as the self-sufficiency of the individual and his or her indifference to external circumstances, although they differed in the forms by which they gave expression to this ideal.

The Cynics opposed conventional standards, defining virtue as the capacity to reduce one's desires to a minimum. The typical Cynic was the famous Diogenes of Sinope (c. 412–323 BCE), of whom many stories were told, including his reply to Alexander the Great who, when he asked what he could do for Diogenes, the latter replied, "Get out of my light!" By practicing extreme frugality, humans could learn to be independent of externals and thus attain true happiness. For Cynics, salvation lies in a return to nature. Later Cynics appeared as itinerant evangelists, bringing their teachings to common people. In their preaching and exhorting they developed the literary form known as diatribe. Though in modern usage the term became confined to denunciation, originally a diatribe was like a homily or sermon, and was characterized by a lively and vivid semi-conversational style.

Epicureanism has suffered from a misunderstanding of its ethical ideal. Epicurus (347–270 BCE) was a far greater person than the word "epicure" suggests. Epicurus distrusted the dialectic and metaphysics of idealists such as Plato. Suspicious of abstract terms, he appealed to people's common sense. Human wisdom lies in the pursuit of pleasure (by which he meant genuine happiness, not sensual enjoyment), and this entails avoiding excess of all kinds. Subject to later misinterpretations, Epicurus's concern was not on sensual pleasure, but on achieving serenity or impassiveness, even in the midst of adversity. The gods, if they exist, live in serene detachment and have nothing to do with human existence. Epicurus had been deeply impressed by the atomism of Democritus, and made it the foundation of his system. Since everything results by chance from a fortuitous combination of atoms, the body and soul are dissolved at death. There is no future for people to fear. Religion, and ideas of immortality, are false. Death brings a final dispersion of the atoms that constitute one's body and soul. Due to limited appeal, chiefly in scientific circles, Epicureanism had little influence on Judaism or Christianity.

The most successful and influential school was the Stoic (see the discussion below and the extended discussion of Stoicism in chapters 11 and 12), which offered acceptable solutions both to the metaphysical and the practical problems of the age. Unlike Epicureanism, which tended to foster atheism and self-indulgence, Stoicism encouraged the development of religious and moral fiber. The universe, according to Stoics, was not meaningless, nor was humanity's place determined by blind fate. Pervading the whole of the material order is divine Reason, and the duty of humans is to live in accord with this Reason or "natural law." The soul is a divine spark or seed of the universal Reason; thanks to one's soul, a person can rise above adverse circumstances, and in the face of difficulties can maintain serenity (hence the modern usage of the word "stoical").

From the earliest days of Christianity, the attraction and interaction of Christian theologians with pagan philosophy was pervasive. On the one hand, Gentile Christian theologians recognized their deep indebtedness to their Jewish heritage, with its historical and this-worldly emphasis. On the other hand, they were profoundly attracted to what we might call a higher spirituality—the soul's desire for higher things—one found in the Hellenistic philosophical tradition, with its allegorical and vertical concerns.

However, if one had nothing but pure allegory and a vertical spirituality, one is gnostic, concerned with rejecting material things and becoming entirely spiritual. Such a stance implies rejection of the Jewish roots of Christianity. Thus, early intellectual Christians attempted to hold together both dimensions—the horizontal and the vertical—but to do so required a non-literal or allegorical reading of scripture.

When we examine the interaction between early Christians and pagans, we turn to philosophy, for ancient philosophy was a form of spirituality, by nature religious rather than anti-religious. While ancient philosophers were skeptical of religious mythology, they were very much interested in the deeper truths believed to underlie mythology. Hence, pagan philosophers criticized Christianity, not for its religious nature, but because they believed they offered a better or higher spirituality. They blamed Christians for being too Jewish, meaning overly materialistic, too invested in natural and earthly pursuits.

In antiquity, educated Christians viewed philosophy as essential to a good education, much as we view the study of science today. Hence, Christian scholars and theologians were attracted to philosophy, and could not avoid interacting with it. The central themes of ancient philosophy were wisdom and happiness, stemming from the overarching philosophical question, "what is happiness?" To be clear, the Greek word we translate as "happiness" did not mean joy or pleasure, as we think today. Rather, happiness meant something like "true success or true fulfillment in life," closer to what today we call "the meaning of life." So the question, "what is happiness?" couldn't be answered by assuming that happiness is what makes us feel good, or even what makes us feel healthy, because such qualities were seen as means to an end, rather than ends in themselves.

While there were certainly hedonists in antiquity, such philosophies were not attractive to ancient Christians. Rather, learned Christians pursued the most widely accepted view of happiness among ancient philosophers, shared by Stoics, Platonist, and Aristotelians, namely, that happiness consists in a life of wisdom. In their estimation, wisdom was valuable for its own sake. Wisdom was the goal of all other values in life, whether money, power, or health; for ancient philosophers, pagan and Christian alike, all cultural values were secondary to wisdom.

To become a person of wisdom required both knowledge and understanding. The majority of ancient Christians, particularly those rooted in early Christian orthodoxy, gave biblical answers to philosophical questions. To the question, "What is happiness?" such Christians answered, "everlasting life," which in the Bible is not confined to life after death, but rather something realized in the present as well as in the afterlife. According to the gospel of John, "everlasting life" is to know God and Jesus Christ (17:3).

Thus, for early Christian philosophers, happiness was the goal of life, and happiness consisted of a certain kind of wisdom, viewed as "the wisdom of God in Jesus Christ." To possess this wisdom was to possess everlasting life, and in order to possess happiness, Jesus Christ was the wisdom Christians seek. In 1 Corinthians, Paul calls Jesus "the power of God and the wisdom of God" (1:24). Early Christians noted that the Old Testament book of Proverbs speaks of wisdom as being in the beginning with God (8:22–31), and they found the same teaching in the gospel of John, where Jesus is called the Word with God in the beginning (1:1–5). Based on such correlation, early Christians naturally associated Jesus with God's eternal wisdom. For them, to know Christ was to know the wisdom of God, and to have happiness was to know Jesus Christ, the wisdom and power of God.

In this chapter we focus on four philosophical movements in the Greek world, all influenced by traditions stemming from Plato and Aristotle, who lived in the fifth and fourth centuries BCE. All four movements—Platonism, Stoicism, Hermeticism, and Neoplatonism—were pagan or secular. All influenced Christian thinkers, contributing to the development of early Christian orthodoxy.

Platonism

Human beings have always been fascinated with the universe, including their place in the order of things. Over time, they devised models of reality to help explain their experience and to guide their conduct. The ancient Greek philosophers were deeply interested in this endeavor, developing cosmological models to explain their understanding of reality. In the fifth century BCE, two pre-Socratics, Parmenides and Heraclitus, set the stage for later thinkers, arriving at diametrically opposite conclusions about the universe. Parmenides, a monist, argued for the unity, permanence, and eternity of reality, declaring that all things in the universe are made of one thing, which he called Being. A rationalist, he arrived at his model of the universe through reason, rather than through the senses, which he distrusted. Heraclitus, an empiricist, focused on change and diversity in the universe. His observations led him to conclude that there is no permanence, for everything changes. As he put it, "no one steps into the same river twice." Unlike Parmenides, whose focus was on Being, Heraclitus was concerned with Becoming.

Two successors, Plato (427–347 BCE) and Aristotle (384–322), championed their concerns, developing comprehensive views of reality. Plato's model, the first grand synthesis, explained permanence and change dualistically. Plato posited two realms to reality, the Physical World, consisting of "particulars" (temporary things such as trees, horses, chairs, and triangles), which are always in flux, and the Ideal World, consisting of "universals" (ideals, essences, or "forms" such as treeness, horseness, chairness, and triangularity), which are eternal and unchanging. Concerned with permanence (Being), Plato viewed objects in the Physical World as copies of forms in the Ideal World.

In Plato's Ideal World, forms are related hierarchically, meaning there are lesser forms (such as treeness and triangularity), intermediate forms (such as beauty and justice), and a supreme form or highest ideal, which Plato called The Good. Using a mathematical model for reality, Plato ingeniously combined the views of Parmenides (Being) and Heraclitus (Becoming), creating a model that demonstrated the superiority of permanence over change.

For Plato, there are two kinds of being, nonmaterial and material. Nonmaterial reality, consisting of forms or essences in the Ideal World, he called "intelligible being," and he contrasted these with "sensible being." Both are perceptible, although not in the same manner. Some things are perceived by the senses, and some perceived only by the intellect. Intelligible things are absolute or unchanging, ranging from such things as mathematical truths to principles of virtue and ethics. They are perceptible only by the intellect. Sensible things, however, being material, are perceptible only through the senses.

To visualize a thing perceived by the intellect, imagine yourself in math class, learning about the Pythagorean theorem. Initially you don't understand it, until finally you say, "Aha, now I get it, now I see it!" What you see Plato called "intellectual vision," seeing not with the bodily eye but with the intellect. What you see, we might say, is an eternal nonmaterial truth, something called spiritual or divine truth. Such truths are not physical, yet physical things can be understood as made in the image of the intelligible form, such as a horse made in the image of "horseness," or a chair in the image of "chairness." If all horses or chairs were to disappear from earth, their ideal prototypes would still exist, for all such "forms" or "ideas" remain eternally in the Ideal World.

As Plato understood them, intelligible forms are not simply abstraction. Rather, they are more real than the sensible images we see with our physical eyes. Sensible things come and go—mere imitations, shadows, or reflections of their forms, which are unchanging and eternal and therefore truly real. For Plato, the eternal world is the real world, and it is nonmaterial. In this respect, Platonists give Christians a nonmaterial way of thinking of the soul and of God. For Plato, the soul (the intellect), originating in the eternal world, has intellectual vision, which is the highest form of reason. The soul is not like the body, material or sensible. Though the soul takes up no space and cannot be seen, nevertheless it is more real than the body, which is changing,

Plato, at one with his teacher Socrates, rejected the intellectual skepticism and moral relativism of his day, which was based on the teachings of Sophists, then the reigning school of Greek epistemology (way of knowing). Led by Protagoras, Gorgias, and Thrasymachus, Sophists traveled across Greece, questioning everything. Believing that humans could not know anything with certainty, they nevertheless viewed humans as the standard-bearers for truth, alone determining the standards for knowledge. Plato painted a rather unflattering picture of Sophists as having no genuine interest in discovering truth, trained only to win debates and make a point. Our word "sophistry," which describes the skill of using plausible but deceptive arguments, stems from Plato's critique. Protagoras appears to have limited knowledge to sense experience, which is relative and subjective because everyone's perceptions are different. Plato's harsh judgment reflects his disdain for Protagoras's famous dictum, "Man is the measure of all things." Gorgias rejected Protagoras's view that truth is relative and declared that truth does not exist. Thrasymachus took this radical skepticism to its conclusion, teaching that truth is opinion, and that individuals should seek their own self-interests by continually asserting their own wishes. It remained for Socrates, Plato, and Aristotle to probe the deeper questions of knowledge.

For these thinkers, humans can know certain things with certainty. Socrates and Plato argued that there are absolutes (norms, ideas, and ideals), and that they are knowable—not by experience or by opinion—but through reason. Truth refers to things that are knowable, discovered through reasoning, using what we call "the Socratic method," a process of dialogue and discussion that asks careful questions and proposes reasoned answers to discover truth. In Plato's estimation, the resultant truth is said to be certain because it is based on his theory of "recollection," that is, on the principle that eternal knowledge is originally within each soul, but is lost when it goes through the "River of Forgetfulness" prior to birth. Reason, these philosophers posited, is the function of the soul, itself a divine spark trapped in a material body.

A human being, in Plato's view, is a dualism of mind and body. The mind or soul is eternal, while the body exists merely as a temporary vehicle for the soul. When a person is born, according to this view, the soul, fallen from the eternal realm, is united for a lifetime to a body. However, at death the soul flees from its physical prison as a bird from its cage. The soul's true desire is to return to its heavenly abode, but before it can return, it is judged according to its moral conduct on earth and then experiences rebirth until it arrives at ultimate release, whence it makes its final ascent to the eternal realm from which it originated.

In his *Republic*, Plato used a famous image to describe the upward journey of the soul to the light of the sun by means of a gradual emancipation from the land of shadows in which we habitually dwell. He considered human beings to languish as prisoners in a cave, where they ignorantly suppose that reality consists of the shadows cast by the light of the fire on to the back wall of the cave. The soul has to be gradually turned around and led up into the light of the sun, to whose brilliant rays it is gradually accustomed.

The sun in the allegory stands for the supreme idea, the idea of the Good, the source of reality and value to the rest of the universe.

In some of Plato's writings, such as the *Phaedrus* and the *Symposium*, the supreme form is that of beauty and not of goodness. The ascent to beauty is less a matter of being led upwards from shadows to reality, than of following the natural attraction each of us has for beauty and sublimating it, so that we pass from the love of beautiful physical objects, to love of beautiful actions, and thence to love of absolute beauty. For Plato, the contemplation of absolute beauty is the highest human ideal. It is impossible to exaggerate the influence of such language on the development of Christian thought and on the ensuing Christian mystical tradition.

Plato's approach to epistemology led him to conclude that the possibility of knowledge, and therefore of morality, is the preexistence of the soul, from which he inferred its immortality. These twin beliefs in the existence of "ideas" (universals, forms, or ideals) and the immortality of the soul were foundational to Plato's religious perspective.

Aristotle, Plato's pupil, seeking unity *in* the universe, disagreed with Plato's dualistic approach, using a biological model to explain how things can change, yet remain the same. Aristotle claimed there is only one reality—the physical—arguing that the form (essence) of a particular thing is within the object. Using analogies from nature such as how acorns become oak trees, he explained that what changes is the matter, but not the form of an object. Building on Heraclitus's principle of Becoming, Aristotle postulated that all things change, going from potentiality to actuality, and that all motion or change originates with a Prime Mover or a First Cause, which he called the Unmoved Mover. For Aristotle, this first cause of motion is itself unmoved, unchanged, and unalterable. Aristotle's "God," though eternal and perfectly fulfilled, is impersonal and therefore indifferent to the world, a "do-nothing God" occupied solely in self-contemplation.

Aristotle's interest spanned many disciplines (logic, biology, psychology, ethics, metaphysics, politics, and art), and while he contributed to each of these, perhaps his single most important achievement was his contribution to epistemology. By dividing human knowledge into several broad fields, he laid the foundation for much of Western philosophical and scientific study. Unlike the Sophists, Aristotle declared that knowledge consists of facts and the meaning of facts. Knowledge includes observation and theory, fact and interpretation. Everything in the universe is a combination of matter and form, potentiality and actuality. The closer things are to pure actuality, the more form they contain.

For Aristotle, at birth the mind begins as an empty tablet, but it contains the abilities of sensation and of thought. Reason, therefore, has the potential to obtain knowledge of reality, but it must do so thoroughly, probing and analyzing until it reaches its conclusions. Thus, by using reason, unaided by any higher power, humans can attain conclusions that are reliable and true.

Stoicism[2]

The word "stoic" derives from the Greek word "*stoa*" or porch, the location in the Athenian *agora* (marketplace) where Zeno (c. 336–264) conducted his school. Unlike Plato, who in his distinction of sense and intellect was a dualist, Zeno and his followers were all materialist monists. For ancient philosophers, "materialism" meant that everything is composed of one or more of the four elements of life: earth, water, air, and fire—all physical things. Light, for example, is said to be made from fire—a material thing. If God is light, which many Stoics believed, then God is a material being. At death, the human soul, conceived as a "fiery breath," returns to God, its source.

The most perfect substance, permeating all things, is perfect reason, which is, in effect, God. The Stoics tolerated worship of popular Greek gods, although later Stoics allegorized the mythological, anthropomorphic Homeric deities. Stoics viewed the world as God's body, and they believed that God inhabits the universe as its soul, conceived as the Logos or divine principle of rationality. Viewing God as the soul of nature, they encouraged people to live in harmony with nature and one another. Unlike Platonists, Stoics believed the human soul to be corporeal, the noblest and purest form of matter. Because all humans possess reason—a spark of the divine—they are equal. After death, all souls, as all reality, return to God, as waves return to the sea.

However, it was by their ethical teaching rather than their metaphysics that the Stoics exerted influence. They were the most influential moral philosophers of the ancient world. For them the end of life is happiness, and this is achieved by "life according to nature." This entails acceptance of whatever happens and a severe restriction of desire to what lies within one's power, namely, one's moral choice. They were non-hedonists, believing that

2. This topic is discussed more fully in chapters 11 and 12 below.

the road to wisdom is a life of virtue free from passion. Mastery of all disordered feelings and passions—*apatheia*—became for Stoics the necessary means for gaining true happiness. They emphasized the natural virtues, such as kindness, patience, courage, and honesty, recognizing that the virtue lay not in knowing how to act, but rather in living according to these ideas. A life of virtue is a life of excellence. One who lives in this manner is wise. A person of wisdom is not driven by passion (by emotion), but rather by reason, by the responsible will. To live this way is to be free. For later Alexandrian philosophers like the Jewish Philo and the Christian Clement, *apatheia* became a necessary stage in the acquisition of contemplation, the ultimate end of life.

To modern people, passion is generally viewed as a good thing, for it is what makes us human and not machines. Ancient people did not have machines, so their greatest fear was to lose control of their behavior, and therefore to act inhumanely, like a beast. In the ancient world, a good person lived according to reason, not passion—freely, not compulsively or obsessively.

Hermeticism

In antiquity, a surprising number of pagans were attracted to a body of literature associated with the divine revealer named Hermes—the Greek messenger god who transmitted communications among the gods and between the gods and human beings—and the Egyptian god Thoth, the scribe of the gods. The basic features of Hermeticism are remarkably similar to the views of the gnostics. According to Hermetists, our true self is our soul or intellect, which is a fragment of the divine. Our true existence is immaterial and unchanging. Nonetheless, we are imprisoned in this world of material change, dwelling in bodies that impede our knowledge of God and matters of eternal truth. Because we are divine in our true selves, God wants us to know him, much as God wants to know us. However, this communion between God and human beings cannot take place as long as we live in ignorance—thinking that the material world is our true home and that our bodies are our true selves.

The first step in overcoming ignorance is philosophical study. At some point, a Hermetic initiate must have an experience of enlightenment (a rebirth)—a vision of or contact with God. Through this rebirth, the Hermetist becomes divine and gains immortality. Obviously, he or she is still a composite of body and soul, still tied to this changing world

Christlikeness

of matter, but the initiate becomes a god by achieving *gnosis* of God and of the true divine self within.

Neoplatonism

The doctrine of the incomprehensibility of God, shared by Christians and pagans, is not a uniquely religious notion. Rather, it has a philosophical component, one developed by the great third century Neoplatonist philosopher Plotinus (205–270), an important thinker for Christian theologians of the fourth and fifth century who were defining the Christian doctrine of God.

Neoplatonism, an adaptation of the ideas of the Greek philosopher Plato, was formulated by Plotinus and his biographer Porphyry (c. 234–c. 305), and further developed by philosophers such as Iamblichus (c. 250–320) and Proclus (412–485). Like gnostics, Plotinus sought to achieve *gnosis* of the ultimate God, but unlike gnostics, this new approach emphasized humanity's essential connection to God rather than its state of alienation from God. Like gnostics, Plotinus believed in a remote and indefinable source of all that is, which he called The One. The One thinks, and his thinking produced the first emanation from him—Mind or Spirit. In turn, Mind generated Soul, the principle that gives life to all, so that all human souls participate in this divine Soul.

Thus, when Plotinus thought of God, he thought in terms of threes. While not speaking of God as personal, he conceived of God as three "hypostases" (a hypostasis is a complete individual being, entity, or divine principle),[3] using a term that profoundly influenced later Trinitarian Christians. The three hypostases represent a hierarchical or descending arrangement, remaining eternally distinct from each other. Yet despite this distinctness, reality is also a continuum, and for Plotinus there are no sharp lines drawn across the map of the universe. The clearest illustration of this conundrum is the doctrine that the soul is never totally fallen, but always remains in the realm of Mind above it.

In his *Timaeus*, Plato had asserted the existence of three primal principles, but he had established no relation among them. Plotinus organized

---

3. The later Latin tradition substituted the word "*persona*," meaning person or mask, for the Greek hypostasis. A hypostasis can be a person, but also a cat, a tree, or anything that is complete in itself. A hand, however, is not a hypostasis, because it is a part of something greater, and not a complete individual entity.

them in a descending triad; from this divine triad, all of reality emanates. For Neoplatonism, it is not quite right to say that The One exists, for the One is Being itself. From The One, all being emanates through Mind and Soul, creating new levels of reality that are both lower than and contained in The One. Everything that exists is thus an emanation from or a level of reality within The One. Everything derives from The One, and everything is intended to return to The One. Plotinus agreed with the gnostics that the material world is not true being, but he did not believe that there was a clear separation between spiritual reality and the material world. Rather, everything exists on a continuum.

Plotinus's idea of the divine Mind—his middle hypostasis—influenced Christianity directly. It is a Platonic element, related to intelligibility. As we noted earlier, intelligibility is what gives us "aha" moments, moments of awareness, recognition, or deep insight. These occurrences are said to be evidence of the divine Mind, which, according to Platonist philosophy, is full of "ideas." Prior to the use of "methodical doubt" by René Descartes in the seventeenth century, Western thinkers did not imagine themselves having autonomous ideas. All such thinkers thought Platonically, assuming that "ideas" are of divine origination. Prior to Descartes, the only being said to have "ideas" was the divine Mind or God. Ideas, for Plato, are eternally intelligible forms, essences, or truths such as beauty, justice, or goodness. For Plato and his intellectual descendants, to know these ideas was not to figure them out or arrive at them autonomously, but rather an intuitive way of seeing. When you "get it," you are experiencing intelligible truth, when time touches eternity. To think this way, to see intuitively, is to experience the divine Mind, which is all-seeing and all-knowing—pure intelligence perceiving intelligible truth.

This way of seeing, however, is not the highest level, for the highest way of seeing belongs only to The One. Our minds have many ideas, but The One, being singular, has no parts and thus, no manyness. One way to conceptualize this way of seeing is to imagine a geometric point—an abstract point without space or time, having no dimensions of depth, height, or width—and to consider all of geometry as driven by this simple, divisionless point. This is a metaphor, but it is how the concept of The One works in Neoplatonism. The One has no parts or division and yet is the source of all the manyness of life, including all of science, mathematics, and ethics—all things are said to be generated by The One.

Christlikeness

According to Neoplatonism, the divine Mind is "eternally generated" by The One—and this is precisely the same vocabulary used by the bishops at the Council of Nicaea to speak of the Son, who is said to be eternally generated by the Father, begotten not once but eternally so. Hence, the begetting of the Son occurs outside of time, meaning that though he came into being, there was "never a time when he was not." For church theologians, the concept of eternal generation was incomprehensible—necessarily so. For Nicene theologians, because the Father is incomprehensible, so is the Son, the Father's equal in every respect.

Christianity differs from Neoplatonism at this crucial point, because for Plotinus, when The One generated or begot divine Mind, it begot a lesser entity, less than itself. Platonists thought hierarchically—what is generated is lower than its source. This is precisely what the Nicene doctrine of the Trinity denies. Though the Son's source is the Father, the Son is equal with the Father. Thus, while there was a hierarchy in the Neoplatonic triad, there would be no hierarchy in the Christian Trinitarian doctrine of God. However, like the Neoplatonist One, the Christian God is incomprehensible because God is not intelligible, having no structure or parts to understand. In Christianity, God would be understood as the geometric point that gives all things definition, yet is itself singular and therefore incomprehensible.

Though Plotinus viewed the body as distinct from the true self, he did not set the soul and the body in opposition. Instead, the unity and beauty of the body manifest the presence of the soul, which animates the body. Like the body, the material world is not a flawed imitation of the spiritual world but the visible manifestation of that world. The cosmos gets its unity and beauty from the divine Soul, which gives it life. As the body is not the true self but a manifestation of the true self, so, too, the true self is not independent of its source. Rather, the self consists of layers of being, and the deepest or most central layer remains in The One. Presently, humans exist both in heaven and on earth, both in The One and apart from it. Describing the One as Being, Plotinus also depicted the One as The Beautiful and The Good. Because everything that exists has its being from The One, all things are necessarily good because they participate in The One's Goodness and receive goodness from The One. Things vary in goodness based on their proximity to The One and on how deeply they participate in The One. Thus, evil does not exist as a separate reality, but is simply a deficit or privation of goodness.[4]

---

4. The doctrine of evil as a privation of goodness became central to Augustine's

Because everything derives from the One, everything is intended to return to The One. Of course, humans are seldom conscious of their connection to The One. Rather than attending to their higher selves, they become distracted by lower, less real concerns. Instead, they should cultivate awareness of the true being at the center of their selves. Aware of this ignorance and distraction at the center of human existence, Plotinus focused on a program of return or ascent in five stages, not sharply distinct from each other. In practical terms, seekers should (1) study philosophy and (2) live disciplined lives that are not focused on material needs and concerns. Furthermore, they should (3) practice contemplation and try to heighten their awareness of the connection to The One. This practice of consciousness and (4) purification, which for Plotinus was the same as acquiring moral and spiritual virtues, leads (5) to fleeting experiences of true *gnosis*, times in which individuals see Beauty itself and stand fully within the divine. As in Hermeticism, humans need not wait for some future moment to return to The One—they can do so now. According to his biographer Porphyry, Plotinus achieved this unitive state four times in his life.

Neoplatonism influenced the thought and behavior of educated Christians for centuries, influencing not only its theology but helping mold the ensuing Christian mystic tradition.

Questions for Discussion and Reflection

Select one or more of the following questions and write your answer(s) in a journal. If you are in a group study, be prepared to share your answers with those in the group.

1. Explain the author's statement that Christianity is a project that grew from a synthesis between Jewish and pagan philosophical traditions in the Greco-Roman environment.
2. Explain the how early Christianity was a religion of belief rather than of cultic act. If early Christianity de-emphasized cultic acts such as Jewish sacrificial rites, doesn't that contradict the emergence of sacramental observances such as the Christian Eucharist, which views the death of Jesus as a sacrificial act performed vicariously as atonement for the sins of believers?

---

doctrine of creation.

3. Assess the merit of Christian exclusivism versus the merit of pagan inclusivism.
4. After reading this chapter, what did you learn about ancient Stoicism?
5. Assess the author's statement that "ancient philosophy was a form of spirituality."
6. Briefly define the Greek concept of happiness and its relation to living wisely.
7. In your estimation, why were early Christians more attracted to Platonism than to Aristotelianism?
8. Why did ancient Jews and Christians find Stoicism attractive?
9. In your estimation, how did Plotinus influence the development of the Christian doctrine of the Trinity?
10. Assess Plotinus's program of the soul's return or ascent to the divine.

7

The Emergence of Christianity

DESPITE WHAT MANY PEOPLE might think about early Christianity, it was not monolithic. It is not so in the present, and never has been. While modern Christianity is widely diverse—in terms of ecclesiastical polity, social structure, belief, and practice—this diversity pales in comparison with Christianity in the first three centuries. During that period, people claiming to be Christian disagreed on most issues, including the nature of God (whether personal or impersonal, and whether one, two, three, or many); the nature of Jesus (whether human, divine, both, or neither); the resurrection of Jesus (whether physical or spiritual); the nature of salvation (whether temporal or eternal, and whether based on belief or knowledge); the death of Jesus (whether redemptive or symbolic, and whether actual or illusory); the nature of the afterlife (whether physical or spiritual, and whether this-worldly or other-worldly); the creation of the world (whether by a good God or a malevolent false god); the authority of the Hebrew scriptures (whether sacred or inspired by an inferior or evil deity); the status of Paul (whether a true or apostate Christian); and the makeup of the Christian canon (which books should be authoritative for all Christians). Furthermore, this summation is but a start to the endless list of items debated and disputed by early Christians.

The variety of early Christian beliefs raises an important question: Why didn't early Christians who held divergent beliefs simply read the New Testament and come to consensus? The answer is that Christians of the first several centuries did not read the New Testament because this authoritative collection did not yet exist. While most of the canonical books had been

Christlikeness

written by the end of the first century, they had not yet been collected into a sacred canon of scripture, a process that would take nearly four centuries to complete. Not surprisingly, even after the completion of the canon, Christians continued to debate its meaning and to disagree on its interpretation.

Christianity had its origins in first-century Palestine, a region of the Mediterranean on the eastern fringes of the Roman Empire. This strategic corridor was vital to the empire, during a time of heightened cultural and religious unrest, exacerbated by economic and political factors. Christianity saw itself as a both a continuation and development of Judaism, initially flourishing in regions associated with Judaism, beginning with Palestine and rapidly expanding to Syria in the north, Egypt in the south, and Asia Minor in the west.

Judaism was the cradle in which Christianity was nurtured, a source to which it was uniquely indebted. Judaism left a deep imprint on the church's liturgy and ministry, and an even deeper influence on its teaching. Until the middle of the second century, when Hellenistic ideas began to come to the fore, Christian theology was taking shape in predominantly Judaic molds, and the categories of thought used by almost all early Christian writers were largely Jewish. This "Judeo-Christian" theology continued to exercise a powerful influence well beyond the second century.

While Christianity initially may have functioned like an appendage of Judaism, by the year 70 it was moving out on its own. The move to independence from Judaism was accelerated by Roman destruction of the Jewish temple and the cessation of the sacrifices that had played such a large role in Jewish worship.

Prior to the fateful year 70, Judaism tolerated varieties of opinions within its fold. Between the years 30 and 70, Jewish followers of Jesus continued worshiping in the synagogues. During that period, it was quite clear that Jewish people began incorporating Jesus into their faith story. Within the synagogues, Jewish Christians were at best an enriching new tradition and at worst a minor irritation. However, when the survival of the Jewish faith tradition was at stake, their level of toleration dissipated perceptibly. Acrimony grew between Jews committed to Jesus and traditional Jews who claimed orthodoxy for their convictions, tying their claims to the belief that the God they worshiped could be found only in the unchanging completeness of the Torah. The shift to a survival mentality set the stage for heightened negativity to develop. After the fall of Jerusalem, many followers of Jesus, both Jewish and Gentile, began to interpret the Roman defeat of the

The Emergence of Christianity

Jews and the loss of the temple as God's punishment of traditional Jews for their rejection of Jesus. Thus, the stage was set for hostility. Echoes of this rising hostility can be found overtly in the gospels, particularly in Matthew (21:43; 23:31–38; 27:25). As rhetoric heightened, the lines around what Jews could tolerate within Judaism tightened considerably so that Jewish Christians, offended by this increasing hostility, began to move more and more into Gentile circles.

From that point on, fewer Christians wished to identify with the rigidly orthodox survival mentality that began to characterize Judaism, while fewer Jews wanted to see any aspect of the Jesus tradition left within their faith traditions. Somewhere in the late 80s a split occurred between the synagogue and the followers of Jesus. We can sense the pain of that split in John 9:22, which states "the Jews had already agreed that anyone who confessed Jesus to be the Messiah would be put out of the synagogue."

Once that split had occurred, Christianity began to move more and more into the Gentile world. Because the gospel of Matthew was written during this separation and the gospel of John shortly thereafter, the Fourth Gospel's blatant negativity toward orthodox Jews (John 8:44) and its descriptions of exclusion from the synagogues reflect that final fracture (John 9:22; 12:42). By the start of the second century, Jewish Christians faded into increasingly Hellenized and Gentile circles, and thereafter Jewish Christians ceased even to think of themselves as Jews, while those who claimed Jewish identity became more firmly entrenched in their tradition. By the middle of the second century there were hardly any Jews left in the Christian movement. "The common ground between Jews and Christians, once so powerful, became nonexistent. This hostile negativity toward Jews and all things Jewish has remained dominant in Christianity to this day."[1]

Religion in the Greco-Roman World

In the Greco-Roman world, there were many religions, including Judaism and Christianity. In the Roman Empire, religion was prominent in society, and virtually everyone was religious. It was rare for anyone to be atheistic. Pagans were clearly religious, as everyone accepted the existence of the gods. Not everyone worshiped the gods, but all accepted their existence. Religion was needed, people agreed, because they knew they were powerless over the forces of life that could harm them. As mortals, they knew they were limited

---

1. Spong, *Liberating the Gospels*, 53.

Christlikeness

in their ability, unable to control such things as drought, war, or disease. They knew there were matters even in their own personal lives that were beyond their control, such as whether their children would be healthy, their spouses remain loyal, or their crops grow. Religion was a way of getting what they couldn't provide for themselves. In other words, people needed someone more powerful than themselves, a role fulfilled by the gods.

Ancient religions were almost entirely polytheistic. Prior to the emergence of Christianity and Islam, the only exception was Judaism. Everyone else in the Roman world worshiped many gods, for their gods were not sovereign, omnipotent, or exclusive. Each god had a role, controlling some aspect of human life. There were national gods; gods of localities (each city had its own god); gods of places (such as of rivers, meadows, and forests); gods over every function (such as of one's home, of the pantry, and of the hearth; gods of crops, of healing and rain, of childbirth, and so forth).

Religion in the ancient world was a way of worshiping these forces, a way of currying favor with benevolent deities while avoiding offending their capricious nature. Worship involved the performance of cultic acts such as performing sacrifices on their behalf and offering prayers as a sign of humility and submission. The root of the word "cultic" in the sense of devotion comes from the Latin phrase *cultus deorum*, meaning "care of the gods." The gods, like humans, had needs, and devotees took care of the gods in order that the gods might take care of their needs. Worship, in this sense, was mutually beneficial. Humans felt the gods' needs could be met through sacrifices, preferably by offering animals or things that were grown, items valuable to humans as well. Sacrifices could be offered in one's home, preferably before one's meals, in the form of a libation poured out or as a burnt offering on a family altar. Larger or more elaborate sacrifices, such as that of animals, were conducted in public temples, many of these places of gathering and worship led by priests and other officials appointed by local authorities to serve as intermediaries with the gods.

Each locale and region had its religious festivals, which citizens and residents of communities sponsored for public well-being. Festivals often celebrated the birthdate of a god or commemorated beneficent deeds on the part of the local or national deity. Many of these festivals were sponsored by the state. In addition to state religions, each region and town had its own god, and it was common for each family to have a preferred god or goddess.

What is common to pagan religions is the absence of beliefs. Believing specific things about the gods was not significant to personal religion. What mattered was that the needs of the gods be met through cultic sacrifice and prayer. It was necessary that one believe in the existence of the gods, of course, and in the obligation of sacrifice, but beliefs about specific aspects of the gods, such as their nature, their demands, or what they wanted devotees to believe about them, these were private matters, unessential to worship and practice. Such things might be relevant to mythology—the stories about the gods—or matters for philosophers to discuss or debate, but they were irrelevant to personal religion.

As odd as it might seem to us, ancient Greek and Roman religions had no beliefs to affirm, theologies to embrace, or creeds to recite. When people went to the temples, they performed sacrifices. They did not recite creeds or confess theological beliefs. As a result, in all religions of the Greco-Roman age, there was no such thing as heresy or orthodoxy, because there was no insistence on right belief or criticism of wrong belief, only an emphasis on the cultic acts necessary to appease the gods. Interestingly, there were no ethical standards associated with these religions. Religions did not establish particular rules of morality. Although the gods were offended by such acts as patricide, they seemed unconcerned with misbehavior such as adultery or cheating on taxes. Such deeds did not disqualify one from worship. Even the gods were known to behave immorally or hypocritically. Such things mattered philosophically, but they were not issues that concerned the gods.

During the second half of the first century, most people converting to Christianity had been pagans, that is, non-Jewish, and it is these people who helped transmit and record the "Jesus material," at first orally, and then literarily. What these people believed about religion prior to their conversion certainly influenced their understanding and interpretation of Jesus, including how they might have modified the tradition they inherited from Jewish Christians.

Pagan religions, as we learned earlier, focused on sacrifices to the gods, a gesture believed to placate or please such powers, but also to result in benefits or blessings. Pagan religions focused on the needs of the gods rather than on affirming specific teachings or truths. Of course, worshippers believed in the gods, that is, in their existence and power, but there were no creeds or doctrines to affirm, and being religious did not require adherence to prescribed ethical standards. While religion presupposed general ethical principles, specific norms were personal, as were matters of lifestyle, more subjects of philosophical debate than of religious practice.

Christlikeness

Unlike Christianity, pagan religions were not exclusive; people worshiped many different gods, and did so in traditional or in non-traditional ways. Because such religions were highly diversified, pagans did not consider their gods as jealous or in competition with one another. They understood the realm of the gods as hierarchically ordered, ranging from the great gods of Greek and Roman mythology to local gods of one's city or town, from gods of specific functions to those of rivers, forests, and homes.[2]

For most pagans, certainly the most literate or best educated, the top of the pyramid was held by one supreme deity, whether Zeus, Jupiter, or some unnamed god. Below this deity were the great gods, such as those comprising the pantheon on Mount Olympus.[3] Below these great gods were various kinds of local deities, who were still mighty, by comparison with humans, but who were not as powerful as the great gods. Below these local gods were family and personal deities, minor in the grand scheme of things, but nonetheless important to individual people, for they were actively involved in human affairs. Below these divinities were lesser beings known as *daimonia*, not necessarily evil spirits but lower-level divinities involved more intimately with human life.

The next level of this divine pyramid comprised a group of demi-gods, that is, humans who were half-mortal and half-divine. Included in this group were people of superhuman strength, like Hercules, or individuals of superhuman wisdom, like Pythagoras, or of superior influence, like the Roman emperors. Hence, imperial rulers were believed to be partly divine. They might have been low on the sacred totem pole, but still supremely powerful on the human scale and therefore worthy of worship. On this lower tier were human representatives of the divine such as Apollonius of Tyana (c. 15–c. 100 CE), the famous neo-Pythagorean philosopher of the first century CE, said to have had a miraculous birth, to perform miracles, and to gather disciples. Even after his death, his followers believed he had ascended to heaven, and they claimed they had seen him alive afterward.

Some pagans might have viewed Jesus of Nazareth in this way, treating him as a kind of "divine person," one worthy of allegiance and even of

---

2. On this topic, see the discussion in Ehrman, *Brief Introduction to the New Testament*, 19–21.

3. Though ancient pagans read the mythological accounts, saw them portrayed on stage or at festivals, or heard them recited by troubadours, most people did not accept these accounts as literally true, that is, as portraying events that had occurred historically. Rather, they viewed such accounts as ways of speaking of traits or aspects of deities, deities that truly existed.

worship. Perhaps among those who converted to Christianity were some who contributed to the canonical gospels, for in them we note progression in the treatment of Jesus, beginning with Mark and concluding with John. Mark's gospel contains no birth narrative and only hints at a resurrection, whereas Luke's gospel tells of Jesus' miraculous birth and ends with a description of Jesus' ascent into heaven. John's gospel, the latest of the four, portrays Jesus more in line with what pagans typically thought about "divine persons." Is it an accident that the earliest canonical gospel portrays Jesus as human and the latest as divine?

Religious Trends in the Roman World

The world in which Christianity emerged, if somewhat painfully, was hungry for religion. Facing hardship, uncertainty, and deprivation at every turn, people in antiquity, in all social classes, displayed a deep need for assurance that life was worth living. In that regard, they longed for assurance against death and fate, protection from evil, spiritual renewal, and union with the divine. To meet this need, the old classical religions had little to offer. Despite periodic attempts to revive ancient piety, the gods of Greece and Rome had lost whatever power they possessed to inspire. The worship of the emperor or his *genius*,[4] fostered by Rome, became increasingly prominent and had official backing. At best, however, emperor worship provided a means for corporate loyalty and the sense that Providence watched over the empire.

In this welter of superstition and genuine piety, two phenomena became prominent. One was the extraordinary appeal of the so-called mystery religions that from the first century BCE spread rapidly across the Greco-Roman world. This is the name given to those close-knit religious groups or associations into which newcomers had to be initiated by sacred ceremonies ("mysteries") not communicable to outsiders. In classical times, the mysteries held at Eleusis in honor of Demeter and Persephone were the most famous. In the first three or four centuries CE, the most popular were Oriental in origin. There were mysteries of Serapis and Isis, of Egyptian origin, and of the great Anatolian mother-goddess Cybele and her youthful lover, the vegetation god Attis. These divinities gained masses of devotees, having temples erected to them at public expense. Perhaps the

---

4. In Greco-Roman times, each family had a personal deity, a kind of guardian angel called a "*genius*," thought to reside in the head of the household.

most widespread of these mysteries was that of Mithras, the Persian god popular with soldiers as an ally of the Sun and thus the champion of light against darkness.

In the second century, during the reign of the Nerva-Antonine dynasty (a dynasty of seven Roman emperors who ruled from 96 to 192 CE), these cults received imperial sanction, particularly when the emperors Hadrian and Marcus Aurelius became initiates of the Eleusinian mysteries and Antonius Pius legalized the cult of Cybele. As a result, senatorial participation in non-Roman (Mithras, Dionysius) or Greco-Roman (Isis/Diana, Serapis/Jupiter) cults increased markedly.

These mystery religions had much in common, including sacred meals, preparatory stages, and occultist rituals, which imparted revelation to the initiates and secured mystic union with the deity. In the rites of Mithra or of Cybele and Attis, for example, initiates underwent a kind of baptism in the blood of a bull or a ram, resulting in the experience of rebirth and the sense of divine protection and eternal security. The appeal of these mystery religions undoubtedly lay in the satisfaction they gave to the craving for an intense personal experience of the divine, with an accompanying sense of release from guilt and fear.

This proliferation of religions achieved a profound syncretism in Greco-Roman times, the gods of one country or region being identified with those of another, and the various cults fusing with and borrowing from one another indiscriminately. In addition, there was widespread belief in the immortality of the soul, sometimes linked with the idea of the transmigration of souls taught by the ancient Greek philosopher Pythagoras (c. 570–c. 490 BCE), and in a future judgment leading either to punishment or to a blessed life with the gods in the afterlife.

The second phenomenon to emerge at this time was a growing attraction, for educated and uneducated people alike, of a monotheistic interpretation of the conventional polytheism. A growing number of deities of the pagan pantheon were coming to be understood either as personified attributes of one supreme God, or as manifestations of the singular Power governing the universe. The current syncretism made this process simple and natural, and at a higher level, it coincided with the trend of enlightened philosophical opinion. An instructive example is Aelius Aristides (117–189), the pagan orator who lectured in Asia Minor and Rome in the middle of the second century CE. Many of his speeches survive, celebrating Asclepius, the god of healing who exemplifies the personal concern of the

The Emergence of Christianity

gods for the well-being of the individual. Aristides's *Sacred Tales* reveals that, although a worshiper of one god, in his view all the gods represent cosmic forces emanating from the one universal Father.

The same holds true for Plutarch (46–c. 120), the biographer, essayist, and Middle Platonist philosopher who, while, adhering to ancestral religious practices and admitting the existence of subordinate gods and demons (*daimonia*), combined this with belief in a single supreme and perfect God. When in 274 CE the Roman emperor Aurelian instituted the state cult of Sol Invictus, he was not merely honoring the sun as protector of the empire, but acknowledging the sole universal Godhead, which, recognized under many names, revealed itself most fully and splendidly in the heavens. Likewise Apuleius (c. 124–c. 170), the Platonist philosopher and rhetorician best known for his bawdy novel *Metamorphoses* (*The Golden Ass*), sums up the matter when he describes Isis as "the inclusive manifestation of gods and goddesses," a deity worshiped across the Greco-Roman world under many forms and names.

During the second century, the church stood at a crossroads. Could it draw clear lines between true worship of Jesus Christ and the era's multitude of Greek, Roman, and Middle Eastern philosophies and mystery religions that also featured revelations from a high God and appeals for dedicated moral life on earth? The answer is affirmative, but the journey was long and arduous before Christian orthodoxy prevailed.

Questions for Discussion and Reflection

Select one or more of the following questions and write your answer(s) in a journal. If you are in a group study, be prepared to share your answers with those in the group.

1. After reading this chapter, what did you learn about diversity in early Christianity?
2. Explain the process of the separation of Christianity from Judaism, including the significance of the events of the year 70 in Jewish-Christian relations.
3. Explain the role of religion in the pagan Greco-Roman world.
4. Explain and assess the notion of a hierarchical pyramid in ancient pagan polytheism.

Christlikeness

5. In your estimation, how did pagan views latent in Gentile converts to Christianity influence their understanding and interpretation of Jesus?

6. Explain and assess the meaning of the statement, "The world in which Christianity emerged . . . was hungry for religion."

7. Explain the role and message of the mystery religions in pagan antiquity.

8. Compare and contrast the effectiveness and benefits of praying to Asclepius for well-being and healing versus praying to Jesus (or, as many Catholic Christians do, to saints such as St. Jude, St. Philomena, or the archangel Rafael).

9. In your estimation, should Christians worship Jesus or rather accept him as human role model and follow his teaching? Explain your answer.

8

The Pagan-Christian Debate, Part I

FOLLOWING THE DESTRUCTION OF Jerusalem in the year 70 and its reconstitution as a Roman colony in 135, Christians continued their claim to be the New Israel, although the issue for Christians about obeying the Jewish cultic laws died out with the destruction of the Jerusalem temple and the emergence of Rabbinic Judaism. Although Jerusalem continued to be an important center of the church in the eastern Mediterranean, it was at Caesarea on the Palestinian coast and at Alexandria in Egypt that the vitality of the cultural life of the church was most evident. These cities were centers of Greco-Roman culture and learning, and in both cities Christians took on the task of coming to terms with the challenges from culture. In each place, Christians developed schools for the instruction of their leaders that helped shape the life and thought of Christianity for centuries.

By 180, a school existed in Alexandria for the intellectual training of leaders of the church, headed by two of the early church's greatest scholars, Clement and Origen. There they pursued the claim that through Jesus, God had brought to fruition the fuller and final disclosure of the divine plan for the human race. In Rome and Carthage, the major centers of Roman culture in the western Mediterranean world, the issues that dominated the thought of the church differed. For them, the central concern involved the identity of the church, specifically, defining Christian orthodoxy.

Important for the church was the developing attitude toward the Christian movement on the part of both the political and the intellectual leaders of the Roman world. Speaking for Christianity were some who had been trained in the best methods of the Greco-Roman intellectual tradition,

Christlikeness

providing reasoned explanations for what Christians believed and taught. The Greeks called this strategy an *apologia*, which means a "rational defense" for one's position (the New Testament also encourages apologetic defense of one's beliefs; see 1 Pet 3:15; Titus 1:9; Jude 3). Four Christian thinkers whose extensive writings provide the fullest picture of this effort are Justin Martyr, Origen, Irenaeus, and Tertullian.

The Gentilizing of Christianity and its encounter with pagan culture were two of the most important historical phenomena of the second century CE. By this time, as the Judaizing of Christianity ceased to be an issue, proto-orthodox Christians came to be seen as a threat to the social, political, and religious fortunes of the Greco-Roman world. As pagans began distinguishing Christianity from Judaism, philosophical Greeks and Romans initiated a systematic attack on Christianity, a debate that lasted into the fifth century and beyond.

The debate engaged some of the best philosophical minds, pagan and Christian alike, a debate conducted on many different intellectual and social levels. Besides the literary format, the debate must also have been conducted, frequently and bitterly, in the council-chambers and market places of many cities, as well as in thousands of homes. Our knowledge of the discussions at these levels is limited, but we know that the debate was not static. Both Christianity and pagan philosophy were in continuous process of change and development throughout this period, and the relationship between them changed accordingly. We can speak of four phases in the debate, associated with four pagan voices. The most substantial critics of Christianity (and Judaism) were the influential philosopher-physician Galen (129–c. 200), who served as personal physician to Emperor Marcus Aurelius; the second-century Middle Platonist philosopher Celsus (dates unknown); the Neoplatonist philosopher Porphyry (c. 234–c. 305); and the Emperor Julian, who ruled from 361 to 363. The most important works on the pagan side of the debate were Celsus's *The True Word* (c. 178), Porphyry's *Against the Christians* (c. 270), and Julian's *Against the Galileans* (c. 362). On the Christian side, the most important works were Origen's *Contra Celsum* (c. 248) and Augustine of Hippo's *City of God*, written after the sack of Rome in 410.

The first phase of the debate occurred during the Antonine age (from 138 to 192), notably in the reigns of Marcus Aurelius (161–180) and Commodus (180–192), when a renewed interest in various forms of Platonism as spiritual ways of life existed side by side with developing Christianity.

The Pagan-Christian Debate, Part I

This period began with the Christian apologists Justin Martyr (c. 100-c. 165) and included Irenaeus (c. 120-200), Clement of Alexandria (150-c. 211), and Tertullian (c. 160-c. 225). On the pagan side, this phase included the satirist Lucian of Samosata (c. 125-c. 180) and the physician Galen, and ended with Celsus's full-scale systematic critique of Christianity.

During the second century, neither paganism nor Christianity formed a closed or unified system. Greek philosophy only achieved a synthesis a century later under Plotinus (205-270), but there was yet little agreement, even among Platonists. Christians were divided into many competing sects, often having little or nothing in common save the name Christian, since there was no authoritative Christian creed or fixed canon at this time.

It is at this point that the debate began. The Christian writings of the first-century had been intended only for fellow-Christians. The Christian apologists who emerged in the second century for the first time stated the case for Christianity to the world of educated pagans—not so much in the expectation of converting them as in the hope of persuading them to call off the intermittent local persecutions aimed at Christians. It was in the latter part of the second century that Celsus responded to what he saw as a threat to the stability and security of the empire, namely, the continuing growth of Christianity that could disrupt the bonds of society and weaken Roman resolve in repelling the barbarian threat. He expressed his views in a book entitled *The True Word*, thought to be published under Marcus Aurelius's reign. Unfortunately, the book no longer exists, but only its reconstructed argument as preserved in Origen's *Contra Celsum*, written about 248, some two generations later.

Galen's basic critique, echoed by later pagans, is summed up in his idea that Jews and Christians substitute blind faith for a reasoned account of their beliefs. While praising the Christians for their way of life, moral and self-disciplined, he finds that, unlike the educated Greeks, they are overly reliant on parables and miracles and appear unable to follow philosophical arguments. When they use reason and intellectual argumentation, it is defective, substituting scriptural faith for logic.

Celsus continued Galen's argument, but, unlike Galen, he was not a friendly critic. He considered Christian faith to be pure superstition. It is clear that Celsus knew the New Testament writings, as well as the claims being made in the second century by various competing Christian groups, such as gnostics and the followers of Marcion. Using the tactic of a scornful critic, Celsus's attack featured a fivefold critique: (1) Christians rely on miracles, which can be equated with magic; (2) Christianity is a low-class movement, appealing to the ignorant and the gullible, who are obsessed with healing and prophecy rather than with wisdom and philosophical truth; (3) Jesus is not divine, but the illegitimate offspring of a Roman soldier. Claiming allegiance to a resurrected Lord, Christians actually worship a powerless corpse; (4) the Jewish-Christian view of God, revealed to a minor race of people and thereby excluding from participation the majority of the human race, is preposterous and unacceptable; (5) the Jewish-Christian scriptures, embarrassing when read literally, have to be interpreted allegorically to cover up their improbable teaching.

Celsus's alternative to the Jewish-Christian perspective was to disavow their doctrine of God, affirming that there is only one god behind the many names. He maintains that there is, and always has been, a single god accessible to humanity through reason. There are, Celsus acknowledges, some admirable moral truths affirmed by Jews and Christians, such as love of one's neighbor, but these insights were already present in the writings of the Greek philosophers, as are the teachings of other religions. Christians are foolish to employ the human, fleshly Jesus as their basis for understanding the divine purpose for the cosmos.

The second phase of the pagan-Christian debate began with the Christian philosopher Origen teaching in Alexandria in 203, and ended in 248, with the publication of *Contra Celsum*, his great defense of Christianity. For Christians, this was a time of relative freedom from persecution, of steady numerical growth, and of intellectual advance. Already, Clement of Alexandria had recognized that if Christianity was to be more than a religion for the uneducated, it must come to terms with Greek philosophy and science. In preparation for a teaching career, the youthful Origen studied under the pagan Platonist philosopher Ammonius Saccas, who later taught Plotinus, widely regarded as the founder of Neoplatonism.

Trained also in Christian learning, Origen developed special competence in the languages and contents of the Jewish and Christian scriptures, so that at the age of eighteen he began presiding over the Christian academy in his native city, Alexandria. By means of allegorical and figurative interpretation of the scriptures, Origen was able to show correlation, as he saw it, between Greek philosophy and the Bible. His instructed his pupils not only in philosophy but in mathematics and natural science, developing an educational plan based on Plato's and not differing in essentials from that of Plotinus. Henceforth, the Christian debate with paganism would be between intellectual equals.

On the pagan side, there were signs at this time of a desire to absorb Jesus Christ into Roman paganism, as so many earlier gods bad been absorbed, or at any rate to create terms on which peaceful coexistence might be considered. It might have been with that purpose that Julia Manaea, the Empress Mother, invited Origen to her court. It is known that her son, the Emperor Severus Alexander, who ruled from 222 to 235 as the last emperor of the Severan dynasty, kept in his private chapel statues of Abraham, Orpheus, Christ, and Apollonius of Tyana, four "prophets" to whom he paid equal reverence. He was not alone in this attitude; about the same date the gnostic Carpocrates was promoting a similar comprehensive perspective, his followers worshiping images of Homer, Pythagoras, Plato, Aristotle, Christ, and the apostle Paul. Unfortunately, Severus's assassination in 235 marked the start of the Roman "crisis of the third century," nearly fifty years of civil wars, foreign invasions, and collapse of the monetary economy.

The third phase began with the Decian persecution of 249, the first systematic attempt to exterminate Christianity by depriving the church of its leaders, and one that might have succeeded had it not been cut short by Decius's death in battle in 251. Origen was one of those tortured under Decius, dying from those injuries in 254. The mixture of the astonishing courage of the martyrs' convictions coupled with the intellectually impressive defense of their faith offered by brilliant thinkers such as Justin, Irenaeus, Clement, Origen, Tertullian, and Cyprian forced many thoughtful Romans to reassess their attitudes toward the resilient Christian movement. By 250, however, Rome faced multiple problems: Persians on the east, Goths on the north, economic woes, and a plague swept across the empire. Emperor Decius felt he had an answer: Rome had lost its ancient spirit, nourished by ancient values. Rome needed a revival of "true" religion, and so Decius appointed a day on which all his subjects would be required to sacrifice to the ancestral gods, followed by a signed pledge of loyalty. A magistrate would attest the certificate. Under dire pressure, some Christians recanted their faith; others experienced torture and confiscation of property; some were exiled, and others martyred. Thankfully, Decius's reign ended a year later, but within six years, Emperor Valerian renewed the persecution, though he was soon captured by the Persians. The next emperor restored personal and church properties to the Christians, and for the next four decades, the church had relative peace.

Christlikeness

The third phase ended with the great persecution under Diocletian and Galerius. A disturbance related to the army sparked the persecution under Diocletian, the final and most violent persecution of Christianity. While some Christians had served in the army, many attempted to leave, while others refused to serve in the military. Some church leaders discouraged combat, espousing love of enemies and other forms of pacifism. The conflict erupted in 303, when Diocletian issued a decree that prohibited Christians from meeting, required the demolition of all churches, the burning of all copies of the Christian scriptures, and the stripping of citizenship for Christians of high rank, forcing all others into slavery. Two fires broke out in the palace, and, as in the days of Nero, Christians were blamed. Prisons filled and stayed full even though pardon was offered to those who recanted. One observer recorded seeing nearly one hundred Christian men, women, and children on their way to slavery in the mines, their right eye gouged out and their left foot crippled. In Egypt alone, thousands of Christians submitted to death, after dreadful torture.

The martyrs who perished in this final persecution gave medieval Christians many edifying tales and legends. Martyrs include Pope Marcellinus; St. Sebastian, a Roman soldier who survived death by arrows only to be clubbed to death; St. Agnes; a gentle girl who refused to marry a pagan; and St. Lucia, a girl of Syracuse who came to be revered in Sweden. The persecutions under Galerius, who followed Diocletian, claimed as victims St. George, honored by soldiers and also by England as their patron saint, and St. Catherine of Alexandria, whose name is attached to the famous monastery at the base of Mount Sinai. All this changed in 312, when Constantine defeated his rival Maxentius at the battle of Milvian Bridge.

The mindset of this third phase was strikingly different from that of the preceding period. During this period, aided by the dismal social and economic conditions of the years 250 to 284, Christianity gained rapidly in numbers and influence. It was in this interval, probably about 270, that the Neoplatonist philosopher Porphyry produced his polemical book *Against the Christians*, which found numerous imitators in ensuing years but also provided many replies from the Christian side. In his book, Porphyry expresses the alarm that is now felt by all religiously minded pagans. He speaks of Christianity as an ideology being proclaimed universally, noting how in Rome the cult of Jesus is replacing that of Asclepius, Pythagoras, and Apollonius of Tyana. Christians, he adds, are prospering, to the point of building large churches everywhere. He does not call for persecution, a

The Pagan-Christian Debate, Part I

policy he abhors. However, his fellow pagan Hierocles was less empathetic. In his treatise *The Love of Truth*, he exalted Apollonius as a rival to Jesus, and as provincial governor he became one of the instigators and promulgators of the great persecution. He was one of the last Roman officials to promote paganism, helping to transform Neoplatonism into a religion with its own saints and miracle-workers. Both responses—those of Porphyry and Hierocles—were reactions against the advance of Christianity.

Similar responses were evident on an even larger scale in the fourth stage, the brief reign of Emperor Julian (361–363). Known by Christians as "the Apostate," Julian was raised Christian, but he converted to paganism and sought to restore the empire to its traditional polytheism. Elevated by Constantius to Caesar of the west in 355, he proved himself adept as a soldier. In 360, when he was acclaimed Augustus by his troops, he openly renounced Christianity. While he did not persecute Christians, he promoted a syncretistic form of religion, restoring pagan education and pagan temples while honoring Jesus among other sages and heroes of the past. One wonders what might have happened if Julian had not been cut down in battle after a brief reign.

Succeeding emperors quickly and decisively restored Christian privileges, some allowing freedom of worship while others rejected pagan worship and emperor worship. The decisive establishment of Christianity as the state religion of the empire took place under Theodosius the Great, who ruled the east from 379 to 392 and was sole ruler from 392 to 395. By 380, rewards for Christians gave way to penalties for non-Christians. In that year Theodosius issued an edict imposing Christianity on all inhabitants. He closed all pagan temples, where possible converting them to Christian worship. In 392, he declared sacrifice to the gods to be treason, punishable by death. Jews were allowed to assemble for worship, but were not allowed to proselytize or enter into marriage with Christians.

It is interesting to compare Julian's critique of Christianity with that of Celsus. Writing in 362, a century after Origen, when Christianity had become firmly entrenched in the empire, Julian entitled his work *Against the Galileans* to show that Christianity was a small, relatively unimportant sect. Nevertheless, he recognized the potential of the Christian message, seeing it as a major threat to his efforts to restore pagan culture. In one of his edicts, he forbids Christians to teach in the public schools. "How can the Galileans who openly despise the old gods rightly teach any of the literature and philosophy of the ancient Greeks?" he asks. "It is absurd that men should teach what they do not believe to be sound."[1]

In his diatribe, Julian claims that Christians have no single admirable or important doctrine, compared with those held by Greeks or Jews. Contrary to the biblical accounts of creation, he prefers the view of Plato, who in the *Timaeus* affirmed that the universe came into being as a living creature, possessing soul and intelligence by the providence of God. Julian also decries the scandalous particularity of both Jews and Christians. If the Creator chose the Hebrew nation alone, it looks as if God cared only for the Jews. He then asks why the God of the Jews should send Jesus and the prophets to the Greeks, having kept them in ignorance for a thousand years. "In our teaching," he writes, "the Creator is common Father of us all, while other functions are assigned to national gods and gods of the cities." He indicates that with the exception of the commandments forbidding the worship of other gods and requiring Sabbath observance, the Decalogue is common to every nation.

Citing the lack of culture and learning of Christians he asks, "Did you originate any science or philosophy?" Then he lists the achievements of the pagans in astronomy, geometry, arithmetic, music, and law. He also faults Christians for claiming to worship one God while worshiping a man (Jesus) as divine along with the Creator God. Furthermore, the Incarnation implies a belief in a change in God's nature, a view incompatible with the idea of divine perfection. In this regard, Christians are in disagreement with both Plato and Aristotle. In keeping with a longstanding pagan attack, Julian regards Christians as poor citizens, who do not honor or obey the emperor.

The Christian Side of the Debate

In addition to creed, canon, and episcopacy, essential for maintaining identity and unity, Christian orthodoxy developed a substantial apologetic literature to deal specifically with external challenges from paganism. Apologetic literature had its roots in Judaism. Such literature arose among Diaspora Jews like Philo of Alexandria and Josephus, who responded to anti-Semitic charges of misanthropy with historical and philosophical treatises that demonstrated how the Jewish law and the Jewish manner of life was actually philanthropic.

---

1. Head, *Emperor Julian*, 76.

The Pagan-Christian Debate, Part I

The essential elements of the Christian side of the debate are well summarized in the writings of Justin Martyr, Irenaeus, Origen, and Tertullian. A native of Palestine, Justin explored the major philosophical options of his day before turning to an investigation of Christianity. He wandered about the Mediterranean world as a Christian philosopher, finally settling in Rome, where he founded a Christian school. His two major writing that have survived are both apologies, the first addressed to a Jewish rabbi (*Dialogue with Trypho*), and the other to Gentiles (*Apology*). In his first work, Justin claims that the new covenant established by Jesus had displaced the covenant with Israel described in the Bible, supporting his contention that the church was now God's instrument to bring the light of God's knowledge to all nations. His *Apology*, addressed to Emperor Antoninus Pius (138–161) and to the Roman senate and people, describes Christianity as a rational search for truth and invites dialogue on philosophical grounds. In a third apology (actually an appendix to earlier ones), Justin counters the false charges that have been brought against the Christians. He notes that the bravery of the Christians in the face of persecution had been an important factor that originally attracted him to that faith.

A major figure among the Christians of the late second century was Irenaeus, who worked to consolidate Christian orthodoxy. Born at Smyrna around the year 130, he was ordained bishop of Lyons in Gaul in 178. Anxious to reconcile Christians in the eastern and western Roman worlds and to establish principles on which such unity might be affirmed and maintained, Irenaeus wrote *Against Heresies*. This major work not only attacks false teaching, but it also offers a full declaration of what Irenaeus considered the essence of authentic Christian faith. Like the philosophical insight of which Origen wrote, faith has an intellectual content that can be defined with increasing clarity. Nevertheless, false teachers who deny aspects of the faith that Irenaeus has identified as orthodox are threatening this unity of faith. Included among these heterodox groups are gnostics, who deny that creation is good or that the God of Jesus is the creator of the universe. To support their heretical views, gnostics produced rival writings to the New Testament, including gospels, apocalypses, acts, and letters attributed to various apostles.

In his definition of orthodoxy, Irenaeus claimed a threefold approach to tradition: the canon of scripture, the rule of faith, and the authority of bishops. In countering heresy, Irenaeus argued for the necessity of a literary canon, a standard by which books could be used to define Christian teaching and practice. He refuted Marcionites, gnostics, and other sectarian teachers with specific citations from the Old and New Testament, indicating which compositions he was using and thus showing which are truly authoritative and which are rejected. Using this method, Irenaeus represents an important stage toward the final formation of the New Testament canon. Unlike the heretics, who take only one gospel as their norm, Irenaeus insisted that there are four, just as there are four winds and four corners of the earth. The one gospel message rests on four pillars, "breathing immortality on every side and enkindling life anew in human beings."

Irenaeus also draws upon the developing tradition of a rule of faith—or creed—to provide a doctrinal framework for Christian belief. Irenaeus's rule of faith, like the Apostles' Creed, presents an epitome of the scriptural story. As such, it also provides a guide to the reading of the scriptures.

The notion of the bishops as the successors of the apostles, already found in Clement of Rome, was argued more fully by Irenaeus, with specific attention to the bishops of Rome. The institutional argument directly opposed the gnostic position concerning secret teachings, secret teachers, and secret books. Christianity has a public creed, an apostolic tradition, and a clear canon of scripture. The consensus of the patristic period, already visible by the end of the second century, is that the unity and truth of the church, represented by the orthodox tradition, is to be maintained by the apostolic witness, the succession of leadership from the apostles through the bishops, and fidelity to an accepted collection of scriptures. These church standards will develop more fully during the conciliar age (the ecumenical councils of the fourth through seventh centuries).

Origen was one of the most brilliant thinkers in the history of Christianity. When he was ten years old, his father was killed during the persecution of the church by Emperor Severus (193–211). Origen wished to follow his father in martyrdom, but his mother kept him safe in the house by hiding his clothes. Trained in both secular and Christian learning, he quickly excelled, developing special competence in the languages and contents of the Jewish and Christian scriptures, so that at the age of eighteen he began to preside over the Christian school in his native city, Alexandria. By means of allegorical and figurative interpretation of the scriptures, Origen was able to show the correlation, as he saw it, between Greek philosophy and the Bible. In 232 he moved to Caesarea, where his program of teaching and writing was so colossal that he had stenographers on hand during his lectures to record his discourses.

The Pagan-Christian Debate, Part I

Origen's greatest contributions were his detailed commentaries on the Bible and an extended apologetic response (*Contra Celsum* and *The First Doctrine*) to an earlier attack on Christianity by Celsus. As apologist, Origen was both a biblical theologian and a Neoplatonic philosopher. When Celsus based his criticism of Old Testaments accounts on a literal reading, Origen interpreted them allegorically, reminding Celsus that the Greeks also allegorized their myths. To Celsus's charge that Christianity appeals only to ignorant and superstitious rabble, Origen makes a strong case for the fact that both Testaments exhort wisdom, noting that this is the thrust of the wisdom literature in the Old Testament. He also cites as fact that while Jesus taught in parables to the crowds, to the disciples he gave deeper, more spiritual meanings.

Significantly, Origen also used philosophy as part of his apologetics, utilizing Platonism as one of his main weapons in the counterattack. According to W. R. Inge, in *Contra Celsum* we find numerous references to classical authors such as Aristotle, Callimachus, Empedocles, Euripides, Heraclitus, Herodotus, Hesiod, Homer, Josephus, Numenius, Pindar, Thucydides, and Zeno. There are no less than thirty references to Homer and sixty-one references to Plato.[2] The Alexandrian school of Christian thought, of which Origen was a leading figure, was instrumental in enabling Christian thought to adapt to Greek philosophy.

Another kind of response to the mounting pressures on Christianity in the later second century was the promotion of the idea that God would intervene directly in current affairs to vindicate the church and destroy opposition. One Christian leader who came to share this point of view was Tertullian. Born of pagan parents in Carthage around 160 and trained as a lawyer, Tertullian converted in 193. Thereafter, he devoted his legal skills to the defense of Christianity. His writings were in Latin, which was a new feature in Christian literature. Until that time Greek had been the primary literary language of the Christians, and Latin the vernacular of the masses in the western Roman world. According to one analysis, Tertullian coined 509 new nouns, 284 adjectives, and 161 verbs in the Latin language. Of these, perhaps the most important is the word "Trinity" (*trinitas*).

In his *Apology*, Tertullian addressed the two major charges brought against the Christians of his day: that they do not worship the traditional gods (which is sacrilege) and that they do not offer the sacrifices for the emperor (which is treason). Instead of accepting the charge that Christians

---

2. Cited in Hovland, "Dialogue Between Origen and Celsus," 207.

Christlikeness

are morally and politically subversive, Tertullian argues that they follow Jesus, the embodiment of reason and power and the enlightener of the human race. As his followers, Christians are the enemies of human error, not the enemies of the human race. Defending Christians, Tertullian provides modern readers with a vivid picture of life in the churches of the second century. They gather to pray to God for strength and guidance, for the welfare of the state and its rulers, and for the triumph of peace in the world. They live according to high moral principles, presided over by elders, sharing the modest resources of the members. They provide support for burial of the poor, for orphans, for the aged, and for victims of tragedy.

Concerned to affirm the continuity of the Christian tradition in the face of new interpretations that were arising, it is ironic that in his later years Tertullian was strongly influenced by the Montanists, a charismatic movement that claimed to have received prophetic revelations that supplemented and modified the New Testament writings.

Questions for Discussion and Reflection

Select one or more of the following questions and write your answer(s) in a journal. If you are in a group study, be prepared to share your answers with those in the group.

1. Compare and contrast the forms (or roles) of Christianity that developed in Caesarea and Alexandria versus those that developed in Rome and Carthage, and make an *apologia* or case for the role you find most important or attractive.

2. Explain the issues underlying the first phase of the pagan-Christian debate. Explain the role and concerns of Galen in that debate.

3. Explain the role and message of Celsus in the pagan-Christian debate, and assess the validity of his arguments. Which of his arguments do you find most persuasive and which least persuasive? Explain your answer.

4. Explain the issues underlying the second phase of the pagan-Christian debate.

5. Explain the rationale behind the persecution of Christians by emperors Decius and Diocletian in the third and early fourth centuries of the Common Era. Explain the role of the Neoplatonist philosopher Porphyry in the pagan-Christian debate.

The Pagan-Christian Debate, Part I

6. Explain the issues underlying the fourth phase of the pagan-Christian debate, and the role and message of Emperor Julian in the pagan-Christian debate.
7. Explain the role and message of Justin Martyr in the pagan-Christian debate.
8. Explain the role and message of Irenaeus in the pagan-Christian debate.
9. Explain the role of bishops, creeds, and the biblical canon in the development of orthodox Christianity.
10. Explain the role and message of Origen in the pagan-Christian debate.
11. Explain the role and message of Tertullian in the pagan-Christian debate.

9

The Pagan-Christian Debate, Part II

WHY WERE CHRISTIANS UNPOPULAR in late antiquity? As we have seen, the evidence points to a number of reasons, in addition to the generalized need in society for scapegoating, that is, needing someone to blame for the ills of the world. Initially, Christians shared the long-standing unpopularity of the Jews. One of the earliest references to Christianity in pagan records was as a dissident Jewish sect that, at the instigation of one "Chrestus," had disturbed the peace by engaging in faction-fights with fellow Jews in the city of Rome.[1] Like the Jews, Christians were accused of being a "godless" people who disrespected public images and temples. However, whereas the Jews constituted an ancient nation with an eminent tradition that entitled them legal protection, the Christians were an upstart sect; being of mixed nationality, they could claim no such privilege.

Furthermore, Christians appeared to constitute a secret society, and, like gypsies today, seemed bound by mysterious intimacy. Like the Dionysian societies suppressed in 186 BCE, Christians were viewed with intense suspicion, charged with indulging in incestuous orgies, a charge that persisted well into the second century. The Christian apologists all felt such charges needed defense. To such charges their antagonists added political accusations. Christians did not behave like loyal citizens. To the average pagan, their refusal to honor the emperor on his birthday by refusing to offer incense in public meant not only disrespect but also disloyalty. Hence the charge that they separated themselves from the rest of humanity, which

---

1. Suetonius, *The Lives of the Twelve Caesars*, published around 120 CE.

The Pagan-Christian Debate, Part II

Celsus brings against them. Celsus faults Christians for shirking their duty as citizens by refusing to serve in the army or even in civilian offices.

Origen's reply, that Christians by their prayers did more to help the empire than others did by fighting, would hardly have impressed patriotic citizens. Of course, there were already Christians in the army by the beginning of the third century, and that situation changed so dramatically over time that by the end of that century Diocletian felt obliged to institute a purge. By Porphyry's time, the charge of lack of patriotism was obsolete, and was apparently dropped.

More persistent—and harder to dismiss because less rational—was the accusation that Christians were responsible for every natural calamity; their "atheism," pagans claimed, had offended the gods. Throughout the third century, when disasters were many and relief-measures inadequate or non-existent, Christians served as convenient scapegoats. In 235, a series of earthquakes in Asia Minor started a local persecution; in 248, a civil war was blamed on Christians. About 270, Porphyry associated the frequent epidemics at Rome with the decline of the cult of Asclepius, and in the early fifth century, the sack of Rome and other calamities were blamed on the Christianization of the empire, a charge Augustine attempted to refute in his *City of God*.

Another cause for resentment was the effect Christianity had on family life. Like all creeds claiming total allegiance, early Christianity was a divisive force. According to Eusebius, writing early in the fourth century, every town and house was divided by debates between Christians and pagans. Nevertheless, in the face of overwhelming prejudice and hostility, Christianity survived and thrived.

In his influential work, *Pagan & Christian in an Age of Anxiety*, the distinguished scholar of antiquity E. R. Dodds notes that the central thesis in the pagan-Christian debate began with the pagans claiming to represent reasoned conviction (*logismos*) against the blind faith (*pistis*) of the Christians.[2] To those reared in classical Greek philosophy, *pistis* meant the lowest level of knowing: it was the state of mind of the uneducated, who believe things on hearsay rather than on logical argumentation. Even the apostle Paul, following Jewish tradition, promoted *pistis* as foundational to Christianity. What astonished early pagan observers such as Lucian, Galen, Celsus, and Marcus Aurelius, was the Christians' total reliance on unproven

---

2. Dodds, *Pagan & Christian*, 120.

faith—"their willingness to die for the indemonstrable."[3] According to Galen, Christians possessed three of the four cardinal virtues, exhibiting courage, self-control, and justice. But they lacked intellectual insight, the rational basis of the other three.

By the third and fourth centuries, the tables had turned, so much so that while Christians now made a reasoned case for their beliefs, pagans began replacing reason with their own forms of authority and revelation. Whereas Plotinus resisted *pistis* and gave his pupils the task of exposing intuitive hunches and subjective revelations, after Plotinus, Neoplatonism became less a philosophy and more a religion, its followers occupied, like their Christian counterparts, in expounding and reconciling sacred texts. If it were to fight Christianity on equal terms, Neoplatonism had to rely on *pistis*, something previously demanded in Hermeticism. As the Roman Empire slowly Christianized, pagans began showing a lively interest in sacred texts and mystical practices. Plato and the obscure Chaldean Oracles became canonized. Theurgy, a type of pagan sacramentalism, became increasingly influential, until it superseded pure philosophy; in some pagan circles, theurgy became essential for salvation. As Christians developed a philosophical theology, pagans developed a theological philosophy.[4]

On the Christian side, the most impressive outcome of the debate was the magnificent attempts by Clement, Origen, and eventually Augustine to produce a synthesis of philosophy and religion, of *logismos* and *pistis*. For example, Origen, like the erudite Jewish Platonist Philo, made far-reaching concessions to pagan philosophy, incorporating both the substance of Plato's theology and the Platonic worldview. Greek philosophy was correct as far as it went, and Plato the closest pagan to Christian philosophy. *Logismos* began supporting *pistis*, allowing Christian theologians to acquire a deeper understanding of doctrine.

For Origen, the cosmos was a living creature, sustained by the Logos, which functions like the Platonic world soul. Within the cosmos are many living beings, including the stars, themselves ensouled, which may provide a future home for certain souls. The cosmos has a beginning and will have an end, but, for Origen, the end will be followed by a succession of other worlds. The grand finale to Origen's redemptive myth is the Apocatastasis (salvation by restoration, when all things return to their original state).

---

3. Dodds, *Pagan & Christian*, 121.
4. Bregman, "Logismos and Pistis," 225.

More striking than Origen's cosmology is his psychology, closer to Plotinus than to the apostle Paul. The soul is eternal; though created, its origin is outside of time. Every soul begins as pure intelligence, and every soul is eventually restored to that condition. However, in the interim, it must rise and fall many times, an idea similar to Plato's notion of reincarnation. Between incarnations, the soul's fate depends on the life it has lived in time. The bad will suffer purgation, but not eternally, since divine justice is remedial, not vindictive. Hell is not a place of torture but rather a state of mind. Heaven, like hell, is a future state of mind, a state of endless growth and wonder, and as physicality gradually changes to spirituality, bodies become increasingly subtle and less material, their final condition probably bodiless. The spiritual body of which Paul spoke in 1 Corinthians 15:44 ("What is sown a physical body is raised a spiritual body") is, for Origen, a temporary concession, for no Christian doctrine was more offensive to pagan intellectuals than the resurrection of the body.

Origen's life reveals a complicated relationship with the organized church. On the one hand he was, like Irenaeus, faithful to the church, an opponent of heretics, and a member of the clergy. On the other hand, he was also like Clement and even Valentinus, dedicated to advanced learning, highly creative, eager to help people advance to higher *gnosis*, and always questioning, unwilling to settle for easy or customary answers.

Origen appealed to Christians who wanted a more intellectual, less close-minded approach to Christian truth. However, he understood that some people find the myths of gnostics and Greeks attractive. The stories they tell explain the nature of God, how and why this world comes to be, and where human beings come from and are going. The gnostic myth is a compelling response to human suffering, oppression, and death, and it offers hope for serenity and equality in this life and in eternity. Thus, Origen realized that orthodox Christianity needed a better myth than that of gnostics and Greeks—a more complete story of creation, fall, and salvation than offered by a literal reading of the Bible. In his sermons, commentaries, and theological writings, Origen laid out his comprehensive vision of Christian truth, refining and elaborating on that vision for the many students and listeners that attended his services and lectures, some of them pagans.

Origen's mythological account of salvation resembled that of gnostics in that it was a story of a fall from a blessed existence in another world into life in this world, and then a return to union with God. However, Origen's story emphasized God's love for humanity and the freedom of human

Christlikeness

beings. God wants everyone to be saved, that is, to return to the original blissful existence, and it seems that this would happen. Origen's story did not make this universe a mistake, nor did an inferior or hostile God rule over it. Instead, this universe is a good creation, made by God to help us return to him.

Origen's bold rethinking of New Testament doctrine was rendered possible by an allegorical exposition of scripture. This art of textual interpretation, originally developed by Homeric scholars and later by Jewish and gnostic exegetes, had long been practiced in Alexandria; from there it was taken and adapted first by Clement and then by Origen. Celsus and Porphyry both protested against abuses of this method, but both were on thin ground, for they used the same method to discover Platonism in Homer.

When Origen wrote *The First Doctrine*, Christian notions of eschatology were in flux, and they remained so for a long time. In 410, when the Platonist philosopher Synesius became a Christian bishop, he professed belief in the preexistence of the soul, doubting the resurrection of the body and the eventual destruction of the cosmos. More than a century after Origen, the Eastern Church Father Gregory of Nyssa (c. 335–c. 395), following Origen, could still reject eternal punishment, holding that all souls will eventually be restored to their original paradisiacal state.

Origen, like nearly all Christians of this period, believed in the reality and power of the pagan gods; he merely transformed them from gods into demons or fallen angels. Origen's world was inhabited by a vast multitude of supernatural beings: each nation, like each individual, has both a good and a bad angel. Porphyry's world had a similar mixed population; what Christians called angels, he called gods. Like Celsus, Porphyry defended the popular practice of offering sacrifice to such beings as a token of good will and gratitude, but this formed no part of his personal religion. For Porphyry, like for Paul and many early Christians, the only true sacrifice is the communion of the individual with the supreme God.

Nor is there any substantial difference between pagan and Christian Platonists about the nature of the supreme God. That God is incorporeal, passionless, unchanging, and beyond the reach of human thought was common ground to Celsus and Origen; both attacked popular anthropomorphic notions as vulgar. In antiquity as in the present, people may call this God by different names, but such distinctions are a quarrel about semantics.

That such a God should take human shape and suffer pain and humiliation was incomprehensible to pagans, as to many Christians. Origen and other early apologists dismissed this by treating Jesus less as an historical personality and more as a Hellenist "second God," the timeless Logos that was God's agent in creating and governing the universe. The human qualities and sufferings of Jesus played an inconspicuous role in the Christian propaganda of this period. They seemed more of a hindrance in the face of pagan criticism.

To many pagans and believers alike, it may seem a historical calamity that Origen failed to win ultimate acceptance by the church. However, literal reading of the Bible proved an attraction too strong to resist. After three centuries, virtually all of Origen's innovations were condemned as heretical by an edict of Byzantine emperor Justinian in 543. It was not Origen but Augustine who would determine the future pattern of Western Christianity.

Paganism's Demise

Julian's attempt to resuscitate paganism by a mixture of occultism and sermonizing likely would have had little lasting success even if he had lived to enforce his program. Pagan vitality was gone. One reason for the success of Christianity was the weakness and weariness of the opposition: by the fourth century, paganism had lost faith in itself. Christianity, on the other hand, was judged worth living for because it was seen to be worth dying for; as Tertullian wrote, "The blood of martyrs is the seed of the Church." It is evident that all pagan apologists, in their polemic against Christianity, were inspired by the courage of Christians in face of torture and death. Such courage was a convincing catalyst for many conversions.

There were, of course, other reasons for Christianity's success, including its exclusiveness, nowadays seen as a weakness, but under duress it proved a source of strength. The religious tolerance that Greek and Roman pagans practiced led to a bewildering mass of alternatives, too many philosophies of life from which to choose. Orthodox Christianity presented one choice, *pistis*, and on the basis of faith in Christ, the road to salvation was clear.

Though exclusive in doctrine and conviction, Christianity was inclusive in that it was open to all. In principle, it made no social distinctions. While catechumens were taught the essentials of the faith, Christian indoctrination required no further education, unlike Neoplatonism. Furthermore, in a period of history when earthly life was increasingly devalued, Christianity held out hope for a better inheritance in the afterlife. Porphyry remarked, as others had done, that only sick souls stand in need of Christianity. However, sick souls were numerous in this age.

Lastly, the benefits of becoming a Christian were not confined to the next world. From the start, Christianity displayed a fellowship (*koinonia*) and community much fuller and more compelling than those of corresponding groups of philosophical clubs or Isis and Mithra devotees. Its members were bound by need but also by generosity and compassion. The church cared for widows and orphans as well as the elderly, disabled, and unemployed; it also provided a burial fund for the poor and a nursing service in time of plague. The love of Christians, not only for one another but also for strangers and people in need, even for enemies, may have been its greatest resource and perhaps the strongest single cause for its growth and endurance.

Questions for Discussion and Reflection

Select one or more of the following questions and write your answer(s) in a journal. If you are in a group study, be prepared to share your answers with those in the group.

1. Why were pagans so opposed to Christianity during late antiquity, and why, unlike Jews, were Christians persecuted?
2. In your estimation, can a form of Christianity exist built upon a synthesis of *logismos* and *pistis*?
3. To the best of your ability, explain the author's statement regarding the ironic change in late antiquity by Christians and pagans: "As Christians developed a philosophical theology, pagans developed a theological philosophy."
4. Assess the logic of Origen's view that Greek philosophy was correct as far as it went, and that Plato was the closest pagan to Christian philosophy.
5. In your estimation, which has priority in your worldview, *pistis* or *logismos*? Explain your answer.
6. What is your view about a person's "soul," and how is your view similar or dissimilar to Origen's view?
7. Explain the reason why ancient pagan intellectuals opposed the Christian doctrine of the resurrection of the body.

The Pagan-Christian Debate, Part II

8. Explain and assess Origen's view that, together with ancient gnostics, affirmed the hope or belief in universal salvation.

9. Explain and assess the similarities in cosmology, theology, and anthropology held by ancient pagan and Christian philosophers such as Origen and Celsus.

10. Assess the merits of allegorical approaches to biblical interpretation.

11. Explain the factors (internal and external) that led to the demise of paganism in late antiquity.

10

A Wisdom Approach to Christianity

As noted in chapter 6, ancient Greek philosophy's influence upon Christianity came mainly from the Socratic tradition perpetuated by Plato and his pupil Aristotle, and it is their influence and debate that energized the developing Christian movement during the patristic and medieval periods. Plato was a complex genius from the fifth and fourth centuries BCE whose work can be read in widely differing ways, but the interpretation of Plato by Plotinus in the third century CE eventually became dominant in the Greco-Roman tradition.

According to Plotinus, Plato taught that ultimate reality was nonmaterial, eternal, and unchanging. In this perspective, the material, temporal, and changing objects of this world are a shadow or illusion, like images projected on a screen or shadows cast on the wall of a dark cave. The realities behind these shadows or illusions are abstractions, conceptions, or ideals that Plato called "forms," by which he meant something akin to models, archetypes, or essences. Thus, behind all things in this changing world are unchanging ideals such as horseness, chairness, maleness, femaleness, and so on, and at the apex of these hierarchical ideals is goodness or The Good.

While Plato viewed reality as a dualism between physical or material change and metaphysical or spiritual changelessness, he focused on the latter, for only eternal essences were unchanging and "real." Aristotle, unlike Plato, viewed only changing material objects as real. For Aristotle, ultimate reality is "material becoming," whereas for Plato, ultimate reality is "nonmaterial being." This debate became assimilated and adopted into Greek and eventually Greco-Roman culture.

A Wisdom Approach to Christianity

Prior to influencing Christianity, the Platonic tradition affected the Roman mind in at least three profound ways:

1. *Dualism.* The Greco-Roman mind was dualistic, in the sense that an enlightened or philosophic mind was conditioned to see the world divided in two, the secular physical world of matter and change on the low side and the sacred metaphysical world of ideals, spirit, and changelessness on the high side. The categories of dualism might change, leading to polarities such as left versus right, conservative versus liberal, or even capitalism versus communism, but the dualistic outlook itself remained consistent in the developing Western world.

2. *Achievement.* Utilizing Aristotelian resources, Greco-Roman culture focused on the physical world and achieved amazing feats of engineering, building cities, temples, road systems, fleets, aqueducts, and other advancements in which they took great pride. Utilizing Platonic resources, Greco-Romans pioneered the life of the mind. Their intellectual achievements armed them with a confidence that their enlightened human minds could uniquely grasp absolute, transcendent, universal truths. Others had messy "barbarian" viewpoints and superstitions, but they had clear perspective and access to objective, absolute truth.

3. *Supremacy.* Greco-Roman philosophical dualism led to intellectual superiority, epitomized in a corresponding "us" versus "them" social dualism. To the Greco-Roman mind, the storyline of the Roman Empire represented the real plotline of history, and other culture had value only in what it contributed to Greco-Romanism.

When the church fused with the Roman state, primarily through Platonic and Neoplatonic philosophy but later also with Aristotelianism, Christianity was transformed into Christendom, a form of Romanism inherently dualist, supremacist, hierarchical, and exclusivist. As Judaism had done earlier, when it "baptized" or "Judaized" many pagan influences, over time, Christianity also "baptized" or "Christianized" many of its Platonic-Roman influences, though it was never able to eliminate them altogether.

When Christianity became the official religion of the Roman Empire, Christianity traded its Jewish heritage to a heritage drawn from Platonic philosophy and Roman politics. As a result, it unwittingly traded its earthly and temporal Hebraic roots for timeless, transcendent Platonic ideals. In turn, theological concepts such as sin and salvation lost their historical,

Christlikeness

ethical, and relational story nature and were transformed into an ideological, theological, dogmatic state of being known as The Fall into sin, a fall from a state of innocent perfection (Being) to a state of rebellion and disobedience (Becoming). This new understanding of reality created a wedge between humanity and deity, leading to a dualism in reality between physical and metaphysical, natural and supernatural, secular and sacred, becoming and being, change and changelessness, earth and heaven, evil and good, demonic and divine, and so on.

In the ensuing church age, writers, scholars, and church leaders now began teaching theories of atonement (salvation) based on concepts such as original sin and total depravity, seldom realizing that such ideology wasn't shaped by the story of Adam, Abraham, or their Jewish descendants, but by the dualistic Greek philosophical tradition that derived from Plato and Aristotle. While foreign to other Greek philosophical traditions, this dualistic mindset also became the social and political narrative of the Roman Empire, of Roman Christendom, and of evangelical Protestantism.

In this Greco-Roman-Christian narrative, salvation (which according to this version requires a transformation from a state of sinful rebellion to a state of innocent forgiveness, justification, or redemption) occurs when an angry God finds a way to forgive fallen and broken humans, themselves caught in a fallen and broken creation, thereby restoring reality from mortality to immortality, temporal to eternal, and humans from a state of detestable change to a state of perfect changelessness. According to this narrative, being forgiven—being saved or born again—means being rescued from the sad story of imperfect "becoming" to the timeless realm of perfect "being," and, like the once-perfect Adam and Eve, restored to fellowship with God. According to this "original sin" paradigm, those who are not saved, justified, or otherwise redeemed are banished to eternal hell—whether to ongoing punishment or ultimate extinction.

As we have discovered in our discussion to this point, the storyline of Christianity may be understood to have developed along one or more of the following paths:

1. As a continuation of Jewish messianism, itself a blend of Hebraic teaching concerning election and monotheism with later prophetic and apocalyptic perspectives. In Judaism, the doctrine of election led to exceptionalism and a binary social outlook, dividing the world between elect Jews and Gentiles. While "Judaized" through purity codes and

A Wisdom Approach to Christianity

theocratic covenants into eventual ethical monotheism, these traditions were also a synthesis of pagan, Hellenistic, and Hebraic elements.

2. As a syncretistic process with Greek Platonic and Neoplatonic philosophy and later, in the scholastic medieval process, with Aristotelian elements. As we have seen, the "Platonic-Roman narrative," later called "Christendom," comprised the marriage of specific elements of Greek philosophy with Roman political, economic, and military imperialism, which led to social dualism and ecclesiastical superiority.

3. As a tradition based exclusively on the Bible—the *sola scriptura* of the Reformers. However, what the Reformers failed to realize or acknowledge was the syncretistic elements in scripture, elements infused with pagan, Jewish, Greek, and Roman concepts and ideals. While the biblical authors "baptized," "Judaized," or "Christianized" many of these influences, they were never able to eliminate them altogether.

Having examined the Platonic-Roman narrative, isn't it time we return to the story in which Jesus would have found himself, a unified narrative in which all humans are brothers and sisters, all mortal and imperfect but all equally under the benevolent guidance of a divine parent called "Love"?

In his 2009 volume *The Future of Faith*, Harvard theologian Harvey Cox proposed dividing the history of Christianity into three eras. He spoke of the first era (from Jesus to about 300 CE) as the Age of Faith, a period of great diversity and vitality but also of suffering and persecution. That era ended when the Roman emperor Constantine invited Christianity into a troubling alliance with his Roman Empire. Thus, the empire that had crucified Jesus now claimed to be the patron of the Christian religion, and the new religion was used to bring unity to the empire.

This coalition marked the beginning of Christendom and gave birth to the Age of Belief, based on creeds, dogmas, and a unifying scripture. The fusion was problematic from the start, and the persecuted minority in league with the empire soon found itself identifying and executing some twenty-five thousand people as heretics. As Cox noted, the religion that was ostensibly founded by a nonviolent man of peace had now embraced the very violence he rejected.

Around the start of the twentieth century, the Age of Belief gradually came to an end, leading to what Cox called the Age of the Spirit, an approach to Christian faith that is attempting to conserve the treasures of previous eras while embracing the challenges of the twentieth and twenty-first centuries. Whatever we call this new era, a new spirituality is trying to be born among those who truly aspire to follow Jesus Christ. It is this new kind of Christianity we nurture in this book, a form of Christianity that welcomes dialogue, compromise, and synthesis with great wisdom traditions, past and present, that will enable humanity to endure and thrive in the foreseeable future.

As we proceed with our study of the role, place, and nature of syncretism in Christianity, what if, instead of a syncretism with Judaism, Platonism, Aristotelianism, or Romanism, we consider a syncretism of Christianity with Stoicism? What would such syncretism look like, and what advantages much such a union produce? As a transition to this topic, we need to establish an ethical framework for our discussion, basing our thought on the centrality of ethics to Christian thinking, living, and being. We begin with the cardinal virtues, a pillar of Stoic philosophy and central to most other ancient Greco-Roman philosophical traditions.

The Cardinal Virtues

For many people, rules are indispensable in that life would be meaningless and futile without them. Goals may be individual and personal, but for these people, rules have to be objective and apply to everyone. Imagine playing a game of football, chess, or Scrabble, without them.

Other people think that the emphasis on rules is mistaken. What we are really concerned about in ethics, they say, are the qualities that we admire in other people and hope to make a part of our own lives. Rules are important at times, but goals and virtues are what we really care about. While rules may be regarded as objective and permanent, in reality rules are constantly changing. What endure are the qualities of people that are worth honoring and emulating.

Both approaches, of course, have merit, and each, taken by itself, is overly simple. Early Christians were familiar with the wisdom literature of the Hebrew scriptures, especially the books of Proverbs and Ecclesiastes, which they traced back to the time of the kingdom of Israel. But they knew that there were similar traditions, some of them thought to be older, among the peoples and religions of the Roman Empire.

For Christian and Jewish writers, the way the natural world seemed to teach this wisdom for living could not be separated from their conviction that the order of that world is the work of God's creation. Paul explained it

A Wisdom Approach to Christianity

in his letter to the Romans this way: "When Gentiles, who do not possess the law, do instinctively what the law requires, these, though not having the law, are a law to themselves. They show that what the law requires is written on their hearts" (Rom 2:14–15). Eventually, this effort to relate common human wisdom to a more basic order established by God in creation took the form of a fully developed theory of natural law.

Natural law ethics, in which basic rules are known by everyone through life's experiences, is probably the oldest systematic form of Christian ethics. These laws are not natural laws in the sense that modern science speaks of the law of gravity, which controls all of our actions whether we think about it or not. Rather this moral law is said to be natural in the sense that it is part of who we are and of the world in which we live, so that its requirements are inescapable. Natural law does not apply to us because we are citizens of a particular country or believers in a certain religion. It applies to us because we are human.

Ideas about natural law become important when people find that they have to live together in situations where they lack shared goals and shared traditions. The idea that some things are right "by nature" is found already in Aristotle, and it was developed by Stoic philosophers and Roman lawyers to suit the needs of a diverse empire. The Roman orator Cicero (106–43 BC) spoke of a law that functions in all places alike because it is written into the structure of reality. As we noted earlier, in the Middle Ages Thomas Aquinas developed a synthesis of Christian and classical learning that clearly connected the natural law to God's decrees.

C. S. Lewis seems to have had this in mind when he identified universal truths in concepts such as the Tao (the Way) in ancient China and *rita* (divine Law or Truth) in early Hinduism.[1] In Hinduism, *rita* is the principle of natural order which regulates and coordinates the operation of the universe and everything in it. Likewise the Chinese speak of the Tao as the essence of reality or the Way of the universe. The ancient Jews conceived of Torah as way, truth, and life. The author of the gospel of John seems to be alluding to this notion of a universal principle of natural order when he speaks of Jesus as the Logos (the divine Word) in John 1:1, 14 and also as the Way, the Truth, and the Life in 14:6.

---

1. Lewis, *Abolition of Man*, 27–29. In an appendix, "Illustrations of the Tao," Lewis examines eight examples of the Natural Law found in legal and religious texts across cultures of antiquity, 95–121.

While the basics of what we call "natural law" may not change, our understanding and application of them does. As our knowledge of the world grows and our contact with people who have cultures and ideas different from our own becomes more frequent, the ability to rethink what is morally required of us in light of new knowledge and new experience will surely be needed.

In the end, neither goals nor rules alone provide enough guidance to show us how to live a good life. Seen as a whole, a good life seems to require more than goals and rules. To have a good life we need also to understand who we are as persons. And we do this by examining morality through our shared narrative as humans, creating a vocabulary of personal characteristics that we recognize as essential to our moral lives. These characteristics we call virtues. Virtues are the admirable qualities of persons that emerge from an examination of their narratives and that shape their moral lives.

So what is a virtue, and how can we speak about virtue in ways that retain the richness and variety of our individual narratives while still helping us to come to a systematic understanding of the moral life? An early answer was supplied by Aristotle in his *Nichomachean Ethics*. A virtue, Aristotle said, is a pattern of behavior learned through practice, so that it becomes part of the way a person normally tends to act. Having the virtue of kindness, for example, does not mean intellectually knowing how kind persons should act. Rather persons having the virtue of kindness regularly do the kind thing. Indeed, the Greek word for virtue, *arête*, can be used for any sort of excellence.

Aristotle's way of thinking about virtue entered into Christian ethics many centuries later when Thomas Aquinas adopted the Aristotelian account of virtue as the starting point for his own thinking on the subject. Virtue, Aquinas taught, is a *habitus*, a habit that displays excellence in action, something done so naturally that it is practiced without prior thought or intention.

To this understanding of virtue, an important corollary must be mentioned. Virtues such as kindness, patience, and honesty require more than just doing something regularly, or not doing the wrong thing; they also require doing something well. This aspect, sometimes known as the Doctrine of the Mean, states that a virtuous action is one that finds the right middle point between two ways of doing the wrong thing in a situation, one being excessive and the other deficient. Courage, thus, is a virtue that finds the middle point between the excessive readiness to rush into dangerous

A Wisdom Approach to Christianity

situations that we call recklessness, and the lack of ability to face challenges that we call timidity or cowardice. Patience finds the middle ground between a hot-tempered insistence on immediate action and a passive acceptance of anything that happens. People who have acquired virtues are not simply following rules. The virtues have become part of their character.[2]

While many virtues are honored by cultures and societies, four virtues were identified by both Christian and classical writers as of special importance: prudence (wisdom), justice (fairness), fortitude (courage), and temperance (moderation). These were called cardinal virtues (drawing on a Latin word *cardo*), meaning that the moral life turned on these four virtues as a door turns on its hinges.

While different circumstances and lifestyles require different virtues, what makes the cardinal virtues important is that they are the virtues that people need to develop in order to live by whatever other virtues are important to them. And whatever virtues seem to be most important in one person's life, they have to be kept in balance with other good characteristics they seek to cultivate. For example, the merchant who practices only boldness and never patience is not likely to survive very long. The same holds true for most occupations and careers. The idea of the cardinal virtues rests on the insight that we have to acquire some habits in the way we live out our virtues in order to have any virtue work over the long run. Those habits on which the other virtues turn are the cardinal virtues, virtues particularly important to everyone's moral life. The identification of these four may seem somewhat arbitrary, but that is because our modern understanding of what these words means has become rather narrow.[3]

Prudence (wisdom) is tricky to understand in modern terms. We are apt to mistake it for merely being cautious, and we tend to look down on those who seem to be too proper, calling them prudish. We wonder how we can make prudence into a virtue that stands without contradiction alongside courage. Yet it is clear that courage can become mere recklessness without some thought about when it is appropriate to be courageous. Patience, likewise, may become procrastination if we are unable to determine when the time for action has come. Generosity can be merely wasteful if giving is not directed toward real needs in ways that show some prospect

---

2. M. K. "Mahatma" Gandhi, Indian nationalist, spiritual leader, and paragon of moral excellence, often observed that virtue is not like clothing, to be put on, taken off, and changed, but rather something woven into the fabric of one's being.

3. This segment on the cardinal virtues is adapted from Lovin, *Christian Ethics*, 68–73.

for solving the problem. Prudence is a habit of choosing actions that will make other virtues effective.

Prudence means practical common sense, thinking wisely about what one is doing and about the likely results. The wise person seems to know when to act and when to seek more information. A prudent person gives generously, but not blindly. A prudent person cares for people in need but avoids making them dependent on the care of others. Wise people have figured out how to live good lives now.

Thomas Aquinas ranked prudence as the first cardinal virtue because it was concerned with the intellect, which, following Aristotelian practice, has priority over the will. Aquinas defined prudence as "right reason applied to practice." It is the virtue that allows us to judge correctly what is right and what is wrong in any given situation. Because it is easy to fall into error, prudence requires us to seek the counsel of others, particularly those we know to be sound judges of morality. Disregarding the advice or warnings of those whose judgment does not coincide with ours is a sign of imprudence.

Justice, like prudence, is a habit of thinking about situations and choices in ways that make it more likely we will actually achieve the good things we intend when we make a moral choice. The distinction between prudence and justice is sometimes difficult to make, but in general, prudence is about the effective pursuit of a particular good, while justice is about the appropriate choice of which goods and goals to pursue. Justice (fairness) includes honesty, faithfulness, and keeping promises.

Justice derives its meaning as a virtue from its primary meaning as the appropriate distribution of things in a society or an institution. A society is said to be just when the things that make it possible for people to have good lives are distributed fairly. Additionally, a just society must assure that persons are treated fairly, including systems to restore justice when it is disrupted.

Justice as a virtue of persons has to do with balancing a wide variety of possible goods to choose the ones that are appropriate. Just persons lead a balanced life between their own needs and the claims of their neighbors, and between the various good possibilities that make claims on their time, energy, and skill.

Justice, according to Aquinas, is the second cardinal virtue because it is concerned with the will. Justice has been defined as the determination to give everyone his or her rightful due. We say that "justice is blind" because it should not matter what we think of a particular person. If we owe a debt, we must repay what we owe. Justice is connected to the idea of rights. Injustice occurs when we as individuals or by law deprive someone of that which he or she is owed.

The third cardinal virtue, according to Aquinas, is *fortitude* (courage). Fortitude is perhaps the most familiar of the cardinal virtues. Fortitude helps us to be bold in the attainment of good and helps us overcome fear and despair. It is the spiritual bravery we need to help us act properly in difficult situations, persevering in the attainment of what we perceive as the good. It can be dramatic, as when rescuers place their lives at risk or when unarmed protestors face down troops and tanks to secure freedom for themselves and others. We also see fortitude in people who face serious illness and death without losing their capacity to care about others or their concern for the future. We recognize fortitude in leaders who risk unpopularity to stand up for principles, or in people who live with dignity in the face of prejudice and discrimination.

While this virtue is commonly called courage, it is different from what we ordinarily think of as courage today. Fortitude allows us to remain steady in the face of obstacles, but it is always reasoned and reasonable. The virtue of fortitude is not the specific acts of daring or self-sacrifice that we admire, but the habit that shapes our choice to act courageously. Prudence and justice are the virtues through which we decide what needs to be done; fortitude gives us the strength to do it.

In fortitude we see most readily how the moral virtues work. It takes discipline to act courageously, a discipline that is built up over a lifetime of taking courage in small things. It takes courage for an awkward fourth grader to face the teasing of classmates or for an office worker to resist the petty humiliations imposed by an abusive boss. Unless we learn to practice such disciplines, it is unlikely that we will be ready to respond when the occasion calls for a sudden act of great risk or for steady endurance in the face of overwhelming danger. What makes fortitude a cardinal virtue is that we cannot act on any of the virtues for very long without it.

Temperance (moderation), like prudence, is also easily misunderstood today. It is often reduced to the concept of abstinence, especially from alcohol. But the virtue of temperance is more than abstinence. Temperance is as much about how we use our minds as it is about how we care for our bodies. Temperance involves knowing what our physical and mental health requires and regulating our pursuit of goals and the things we desire so that everything we do contributes to our long-term well-being. Temperance

Christlikeness

involves knowing our limits and enjoying each good thing in a way that enables us to enjoy other good things in the future. The temperate person knows how to change and grow spiritually, always remaining open to explore new possibilities. Temperate people participate fully in the opportunities and experiences that are available now, but in ways that keep them available for new experiences and for the needs of others in the future.

Temperance, Aquinas declared, is the fourth and final cardinal virtue. While fortitude is concerned with the restraint of fear so that we can act, temperance is the restraint of our desires or passions. Food, drink, and sex are all necessary for our survival, individually and as a species, yet a disordered desire for any of these goods can have disastrous consequences, physical and moral. Temperance is the virtue that attempts to keep us from excess. Temperance is the "golden mean" that helps keep our passion from ruling over reason. The idea is to avoid excessive behavior so that such acts do not dominate or distract from what will make us ultimately most happy.

We have addressed the natural virtues before the supernatural virtues for a reason. The natural leads to the spiritual, but the spiritual arises out of the physical. This principle is basic to all spirituality, for healthy spirituality is holistic. Bodily health, mental health, and emotional health are not peripheral to spirituality; rather, they are the lifeblood of soulwork. As body is to mind, mind to soul, and soul to Spirit, so the natural is prerequisite to the supernatural.

Questions for Discussion and Reflection

Select one or more of the following questions and write your answer(s) in a journal. If you are in a group study, be prepared to share your answers with those in the group.

1. Explain the effect of Platonic and Neoplatonic influences upon Roman cultures.
2. Explain the role syncretism played in early, medieval, and reformation phases of Christian history.
3. Explain the benefits or advantages for the development of a new kind of Christianity in Cox's Age of the Spirit.
4. This chapter discusses the value of rules, goals, and virtues. How do these differ? Give an example of a rule, a goal, and a virtue. In your

estimation, which of these comes first in terms of priority? Does the order differ in priority depending on whether you are thinking of their role individually or for society?

5. When you think of the ethical rules or behavioral values in your life, do you see them as originating with God, in nature, or in society? Explain your answer.

6. Do you consider certain ethical norms universal in application, meaning that they are normative for all humans? If so, list your top three natural laws.

7. What commonality do you find in the Chinese Tao, the Hindu *rita*, and the Jewish Torah? Can you think of a Christian counterpart to these?

8. Describe the Doctrine of the Mean. Do you find this principle to be operative in your life? Explain your answer.

9. In your own words, describe "prudence" as an ethical norm. Why did Thomas Aquinas rank it first among the cardinal virtues? How would you rank the cardinal virtues? Explain your answer.

10. How is fortitude different from courage? Give examples of each, either from your own life or from the example of others.

11. Modern individuals exhibit particular problems dealing with addictive behavior. Give specific examples of how temperance can help you to avoid excessive behavior.

11

The Storyline of Stoicism

WHEN PEOPLE THINK OF Stoicism or of stoic values, they commonly think its practitioners march through life with a stiff upper lip, suppressing their emotions and enduring adversity. While endurance is a Stoic value, Stoics are not staunch legalists or puritanically motivated, and they certainly don't try to suppress their emotions. When we read the work of the Stoics, we encounter individuals who are cheerful and optimistic about life and who are fully enjoying life's pleasures. The goal of Stoics is not to banish emotion from life but rather to banish negative emotions such as anger, grief, anxiety, and fear, and to enhance positive emotions such as love, peace, joy, and tranquility. And instead of passive resignation to the world's injustice, modern Stoics are fully engaged in life, working hard to make the world a better place. They don't worry about the thing they can't control, but rather focus on the things they can control.

As noted earlier, Stoicism is an ancient Greco-Roman philosophy of life analogous in scope to philosophies or religions like Buddhism, Confucianism, or Christianity. Ancient Stoics defined philosophy comprehensively as "the knowledge of things divine and human." Their goal was to help people navigate everyday existence and the challenges it might pose, as well as to help them reflect on the broader meaning and direction of their lives. Likewise, modern Stoicism helps us decide on our priorities, on how we interact with our fellow human beings, and on how we face the inevitable setbacks of life and finally face our own mortality. These are some of the issues that Stoicism helps us address in the pursuit of what the ancients called a eudaimonic life, that is, a life that is worth living because it has moral excellence as its ultimate goal. To accomplish that end, classic Stoic pedagogy helped pupils explore the study of "physics," "logic," and "ethics."

The reason we place these terms in quotation marks is because Stoics meant something far broader than their contemporary meaning. "Physics" meant the study of all the natural sciences and metaphysics, focusing on how the world works. "Logic" meant the study of anything that might improve one's reasoning, including formal logic, epistemology, rhetoric, and what we today call cognitive science. And "ethics" meant not just the study of right and wrong actions but an understanding of how to live one's life. Stoics taught that in order to live a good life, people should reason correctly and act in accordance with a working understanding of how things are. No action, however reasonable and well justified, is right unless it is done from a virtuous disposition. Accordingly, only a virtuous person can perform a right action, and only a wise person has virtue. For Stoics, the wise person is guided by *apatheia* or freedom from passion. They consider passion as the behavior of fools, as an irrational and excessive movement of the soul guided by a seriously incorrect view about the value of a situation or thing, often driven by negative emotions such as grief and misguided desire. The Stoic view seems to be that confusion about the kind of value things have lies at the heart of our tendency to unhealthy emotional reactions. The ideal state of mind, then, is not the absolute unfeeling condition suggested by the term "stoical," but an affective life characterized by stable and healthy emotional reactions to events.

While Stoicism is often portrayed as harsh and unfeeling, its followers insist that it is a liberating, joyous way of life, based on the attainment of tranquility, which in turn makes it easier to pursue virtue. Founded by the Cypriot philosopher Zeno of Citium (344–262 BCE), Stoicism has many adherents to this day. The Stoics of ancient Greece considered themselves to be the heirs of Socratic moral philosophy and the natural philosophy of the pre-Socratic Heraclitus of Ephesus (sixth century BCE).

Heraclitus is perhaps most famous for having said that one cannot step into the same river twice. What he meant by this is that everything in the universe is constantly changing and therefore cannot be the same today as yesterday. This approach regards dynamic change, and not static changeless truth, as the fundamental aspect of reality. Nowadays, it is called process metaphysics, which happens to be in line with the latest research in fundamental physics. The Stoics developed their metaphysics on the basis of Heraclitus's insight, and used the notion of impermanence as a way to counter our natural tendency to resist change.

The Stoics naturally felt indebted to Socrates, having adopted and developed his notion that philosophy ought to be practiced, not just studied, as well as the idea that virtue is the chief good. Until Socrates, philosophers had been interested in the theoretical exploration of many areas of inquiry, including metaphysics (what we call religion) and natural philosophy (what we call science). But their interest in practicing a particular way of living was minimal at best. Socrates represented a turning point. He spent most of his life in Athens, talking to whomever would listen, inquiring whether they knew what they meant when they used words such as justice, piety, truth, good, and the like. Socrates lived an ethical life, paying attention to what he was doing and why, and trying to be the best human being he could be.

Plato, who was Socrates' student, and Aristotle, who was Plato's student, did not follow in Socrates's footsteps. Rather than engage in the practical exercise of philosophy, they returned to general theoretical inquiries. During the Hellenistic period (the period from Alexander the Great [356–323 BCE] to the battle of Actium[1] in 31 BCE, various schools of philosophy flourished, including three virtue-based philosophies: Peripateticism, Cynicism, and Stoicism. These featured a decided turn toward the Socratic way: philosophy as the art of living. The Stoics, in particular, took the Socratic approach and married it with that of the pre-Socratics. That is to say, they studied subjects outside ethics, such as logic and metaphysics, but only with the goal of figuring out how to live a eudaimonic life. Their rationale was that if one doesn't know how to reason about things—or does not appreciate how the world works—then one is likely to mislive.

The Peripatetics, followers of Aristotle, believed that virtue is sufficient for *eudaimonia*, but it was not enough. For Aristotle, to live well one also needs essential external goods like shelter, good health, and friends. A virtuous person could be the victim of a tragedy that leaves him or her ill, homeless, or alone, and so despite his or her good character, their life would not have gone well; they had failed to attain *eudaimonia*. In order to flourish, human beings required a certain degree of material comfort.

The Cynics, likewise, believed that virtue is both necessary and sufficient, but unlike the Peripatetics, they maintained that externals actually

---

1. The battle of Actium was a decisive naval confrontation between the forces of Octavian on one side and Mark Antony and Cleopatra on the other. Octavian won, ending the Roman civil war that had persisted since the death of Julius Caesar some thirteen years earlier, becoming the first Roman emperor with the name of Caesar Augustus.

get in the way. Accordingly, they did not marry or have children, did not own property, and spent most of their time reminding others people that they were not living fully.

The Stoics struck a brilliant compromise between the rather comfortable Peripatetics and the austere Cynics. Like Cynics, Stoics thought that virtue is both necessary and sufficient for a eudaimonic life. In agreement with Aristotle, they maintained that externals add practical value, but should be regarded with indifference. Being wealthy, educated, or healthy, however, do not make one a good person, but being poor, uneducated, or sick do not make one a bad person. Even if virtuous people suffer multiple tragedies or endure intense physical torture, they still have a chance at *eudaimonia* because these external things need not corrupt their virtuous character. Once a person become virtuous, nothing can ruin his or her life. For the Stoics, virtue is the limit of happiness. The famous Stoic philosopher emperor Marcus Aurelius asks in his *Meditations*, "How can that which does not make a person worse, make the life of a person worse?" The obvious Stoic answer is: it can't. Only virtue is good, and vice is bad, and everything else is indifferent.

The Cynics thought that only virtue is good, and all other so-called goods ought to be scorned and actively avoided. The best life was a rigidly austere life of poverty and extreme asceticism. Stoicism, on the other hand, says that we should not scorn externals, but regard them with indifference. The demands of virtue still require that we take care of ourselves and others, and the Stoics believe that such things can be choice-worthy without also being taken as ultimate ends.

Stoics think that one should not be blamed for things outside one's control. A favorite example that ancient Stoics gave to illustrate this point is the "archer metaphor." A good archer does all that he can to hit his target. But once he lets go of the bowstring, it is no longer in his power to ensure that the arrow hits the target. A sudden gust of wind could blow the arrow off course, or something could intercept the arrow before it hits the target. Nevertheless, the archer is a good archer if he does everything in his power to hit the target. Although the archer aids at the target, the target is not his goal. It is not hitting the target that makes an archer a good archer, but rather doing all he can to be a good archer. This means he must try his best to hit the target, while regarding hitting the target as indifferent to his ultimate goal.

Christlikeness

Stoics understand that everyone exists to help each other, and that everything exists to help everything else. Because of this, they are able to make their own choices without fear of divine punishment or favor. They fear nothing because there is nothing that can hurt them that was not designed by nature itself. Living according to nature, this second pillar of Stoic philosophy, known as the dichotomy of control, was famously summarized by the slave-turned-teacher Epictetus at the beginning of his manual for a good life, *The Enchiridion*. While we can influence our body, things such as property, reputation, and office ultimately are not under our power. Even the healthiest body can be struck by disease or accident. Our property can be taken away for a number of reasons beyond our control. And our reputation can be ruined through gossip and other people's malicious intent. By contrast, opinion, motivation, desire, aversion, and other things may be influenced by others, but ultimately, they are our responsibility. If we take the dichotomy of control to heart, we can change our entire outlook on life. We no longer need to focus on the outcomes of our decisions but instead with their soundness. The outcome is not up to us, but the decision to do certain things rather than others certainly is.

The natural, wholesome, and helpful way of life Stoics choose is supported by seven holistic ways of thinking, acting, and living:

1. They don't worry about things over which they have no control. They put things into two buckets: what they can control and what they cannot control. They act on the things they can control and accept the things they cannot.
2. They don't allow themselves to be taken by surprise, and they don't allow themselves to get upset over things that occur naturally.
3. They don't panic when things go wrong, and they remain calm in the face of chaos, for they know that getting upset only makes things worse. So they remain at ease, accept things as they are, and get to work on a solution.
4. They are happy with what they have. They keep life simple, realizing they already have everything that truly matters.
5. They accept everything that happens. They focus on how they can influence the future, but they accept the present moment as it is.
6. They listen more than they speak. While valuing conversations, they listen intently, knowing they learn best by listening.

7. They do not fear death. Rather than avoid the topic, they take time to reflect upon their mortality, knowing that such reflection helps them to appreciate their life and the present moment that much more.

Ancient Stoicism

The story of how Zeno, a Phoenician from Cyprus, became a philosopher is both interesting and instructive. On board a merchant ship sailing in the Aegean Sea near Athens, Zeno was one of the few passengers who survived the effects of a powerful storm, which sank the ship with all its cargo and many people aboard. After recovering from the profound shock of this experience, he entered a bookshop where he listened to the reading of Xenophon's account of the famous Athenian philosopher Socrates. Fascinated by Socrates's life, he resolved to become a philosopher. Turning to the bookseller, he asked where he could find a philosopher. The bookseller looked out and saw the notable philosopher Crates of Thebes walking by and soon Zeno became his student. After a few years of studying with a number of teachers, Zeno felt ready to begin his own school of practical philosophy, which became known as Stoicism, named for the *Stoa Poikile* (Painted Porch), a colonnade decorated with murals located in the middle of the Athenian marketplace where people gathered frequently.

The basic ideas of Stoicism, listed below, are rooted in Zeno's experience during and after the shipwreck, as well as in what he learned by studying philosophy as taught by other schools:

1. We do not control as much as we think we do about the world and our lives, as the sudden shipwreck demonstrated.
2. We can recover from disasters by focusing on what is in our power, like Zeno changing his profession from merchant to philosopher.
3. Following the example of Socrates, the most important thing in life is to live in the light of reason as a good member of the human community, rather than to pursue wealth and fame.

Zeno's approach to ethics is known as "virtue ethics," which focuses on the character of an individual, on how one becomes a better person, rather than on standard ethics, which focuses on actions, whether they are right or wrong. Virtue ethics characterized the approach of Aristotle, who saw the goal of ethics to be *eudaimonia*. While this Greek word has no direct

Christlikeness

English translation, it is often rendered as "happiness" but is best translated as "human flourishing," in settings where peace, love, and joy prevail. The Stoics agreed with Aristotle's definition of *eudaimonia* as "activity of the soul in accordance with virtue." The Greek word for virtue is *arête*, a word meaning "excellence." For Aristotle, *arête* is a quality that makes an action or a person excellent. For example, a good knife is a sharp knife. Therefore, one of the "virtues" of a knife is its sharpness. For humans, virtue is a state of character, which makes humans good at being humans. As Aristotle made clear, good humans are rational and social beings. In antiquity, the list of virtues often varied from school to school and philosopher to philosopher, but most schools of ancient thought agreed on the four cardinal virtues of prudence (wisdom), temperance (moderation or self-control), courage (not simply physical but moral; the courage to stand up and do the right thing), and justice (the wisdom to know the right thing to do in most any situation).

Distilled to its essence, Stoicism is a philosophy of personal betterment that puts an emphasis on living reasonably and cooperatively with others, and provides emotional ballast against the vicissitudes of fortune and pain alike. Ultimately, Stoicism encourages people to govern their lives from within, according to their own moral compass, rather than being pushed around by external forces and factors. Based on these observations, Stoics conclude that a life well lived is one in which individuals deploy reason for the improvement of society. Living naturally means using our brains and our hearts to make life on this planet better for everyone, and therefore for ourselves.

After Zeno, the second head of the Stoa was Cleanthes, an impoverished boxer who worked as a water carrier by night in order to study philosophy by day. He was succeeded by Chrysippus, a prolific writer and brilliant logician who is primarily responsible for the Stoic philosophy as we understand it today. Had his work survived, he would likely be as much a household name as Plato and Aristotle. In the year 86 BCE, the Roman general Sulla defeated the Athenians, greatly altering the course of Western philosophy in general and Stoicism in particular. Philosophers moved to other places in the Mediterranean world, including Alexandria in Egypt, the Greek island of Rhodes, and Rome, leading to a period called the Middle Stoa.

The two major figures of this period were Panaetius of Rhodes and his pupil Posidonius. Panaetius inquired into such ideas as how to reconcile the apparent conflict between what is moral and what is useful. However,

The Storyline of Stoicism

Stoicism was developed most fully by Posidonius (c. 135–c. 51 BCE), the last truly original Greek thinker, who constructed a system combining Stoic and Platonic thought that would become the dominant philosophy of the later Hellenistic age. Posidonius was a natural philosopher—or scientist, in modern terminology—who took seriously the Stoic notion that everything is interconnected. He studied astronomy, meteorology, geography, geology, and ethnology.

In this period, the original pantheistic doctrine of God was modified in two directions: on the one hand, a greater measure of transcendence was allowed to God, while on the other hand, Posidonius admitted some hope of immortality, and least for the great and good. Admission of partial immortality opened the way for a more general hope, such as was offered by the mystery religions. Stoicism would also provide the vocabulary of the thought of Philo of Alexandria, the Jewish thinker who read the philosophy of Posidonius into the Old Testament.

The intellectual energy of Panaetius and Posidonius had no rivals. In their time and through their influence, Stoicism was introduced to the Romans, among whom it was to have its greatest success. By the end of the first century BCE, Stoicism was without doubt the predominant philosophy among the Romans, and references to Stoic doctrines are common in Latin literature. Likewise, in the Greek world of the first two centuries CE, Stoicism remained a lively influence.

The last ancient period of Stoic history is the best understood and most influential, since many of the writings from that time survive. This is the time of such Stoic thinkers as Seneca, (a contemporary of Paul), Musonius Rufus, Hierocles, Epictetus, and the Roman emperor Marcus Aurelius. The ethical teachings of these later Stoics contain superb examples of moral wisdom. However, since Stoics do not believe in a personal God, their creed, though noble and elevated, remained a philosophy and never made a religious appeal to the masses.

The Influence of Stoicism on Christianity and Later Western Thinkers

After the death of Marcus Aurelius in 180 CE, Stoicism declined, along with all the Greco-Roman philosophical schools. The peaceful and prosperous age of the Antonines (138–180) was succeeded by war and political and economic woes. New religions, and for the philosophically inclined a

Christlikeness

revived Platonism, offered the consolation of life after death for the trials of this world. These factors made way for the rise of Christianity, which was embraced by the emperor Constantine in the year 312 CE. During the first Christian centuries Stoicism influenced numerous Christian writers, including Paul of Tarsus, Augustine of Hippo, and Thomas Aquinas. The apostle Paul was rumored to have corresponded with the Roman Stoic philosopher Seneca, though correspondence to that effect turned out to be a forgery. Nevertheless, according to the New Testament book of Acts, Paul arrived in Athens and interacted with Epicurean and Stoic philosophers. In the fourth and early fifth centuries, Augustine was influenced by Stoic ethics, logic, and physics. However, his disagreement with Stoicism shaped Christian theology and the reception of Stoic philosophy through the centuries.

During the thirteenth century, Dominican friar Thomas Aquinas—dubbed *the* Christian theologian by the Counter-Reformation Council of Trent—borrowed wholesale from Stoic philosophy when he combined the four cardinal Stoic virtues with the more typical theological (supernatural) virtues of faith, hope, and charity (love).[2]

Stoicism came back into vogue during the Renaissance and the Enlightenment, influencing such figures as Descartes, Rousseau, Hume, and Adam Smith, among others. Perhaps the most important early modern philosophers to be strongly affected by Stoic beliefs and values was Baruch Spinoza (1632–1677), who equated the world or Nature with God, a metaphysical position similar to that of the Stoics. According to Spinoza, everything happens through cause and effect, which means that everything that happens stems from God or Nature. Another major Enlightenment figure to be influenced by Stoicism was the German philosopher Immanuel Kant (1724–1804). While his deontological—that is, duty-based—system of ethics is quite different from the virtue ethics of Stoicism, Kant admired the Stoic emphasis on one's duty toward oneself and others, as well as the Stoic notion of cosmopolitanism.

The nineteenth-century American transcendentalists Ralph Waldo Emerson (1803–1882) and henry David Thoreau (1817–1869) are also associated with Stoicism. Emerson's essay "Self-Reliance," published in 1841, features strong echoes of Seneca and Marcus Aurelius. Thoreau also

---

2. The topic of the theological or supernatural virtues is discussed at length in chapter 13 below.

embraced many aspects of the Stoic approach, particularly the notion that philosophy ought to be practical.

Of particular importance to our study is the work of the Flemish Renaissance philosopher Justus Lipsius in the sixteenth and early seventeenth centuries, whose works sought to combine the beliefs of Stoicism and Christianity. The philosophical movement, which came to be known as Neostoicism, took on the nature of religious syncretism. Lipsius maintained that human beings should not submit to the negative physical passions, called "the flesh" or the "old self" by New Testament writers such as Paul (see Romans 6:6; 7:5, 14; 8:4, 12), but rather to God. He also argued that human freedom consists in submitting to the will of God. This is a Christian twist on the Stoic notion that freedom comes from accepting whatever the universe throws our way.

After Lipsius, Neostoicism failed to attract a significant following, although it continues to this day among Roman Catholic authors such as Léontine Zanta and Julien-Eymard d'Angers. According to John Sellars, "a Neostoic is a Christian who draws on Stoic ethics, but rejects those aspects of Stoic materialism and determinism that contradict Christian teaching."[3] To examine the possibility of a synthesis or correlation of Christianity with Stoicism, we begin with the Stoic view of God.

Do Stoics Believe in God?

Monotheism was attractive in the Hellenistic world, and the teachings of philosophical schools such as Stoicism pointed away from the many gods of Greek and Roman mythology and toward the unifying power of a supreme being. By the time of Jesus, the teachings of Greek schools of philosophy such as Stoicism had come to emphasize the universal nature of truth and the unifying character of divine reality. The book of Acts recalls Paul in Athens as having quoted the Stoic philosopher Aratus, who had said that all human beings are God's offspring (Acts 17:28). Like Paul, the Stoic philosopher Seneca (4 BCE–c. 65 CE) had emphasized the pervasive presence of God in the natural realm as well as in personal experience. In his *Moral Epistles* Seneca wrote, "God is near you, he is with you, he is in you" (41.1).

One of the most striking features of Stoic theology was its rather fluid conception of God. Most ancient Stoics were pantheists, for they believed that God in intrinsic to—and inherent in—the world. However, most were

3. Sellars, *Stoicism*, 144.

Christlikeness

also polytheists and monotheists as well, for they often used the terms "god" and "gods" interchangeably; As they understood nature, the entire universe is a living organism endowed with reason or logos. And they referred to this living organism interchangeably as God or Nature. If the universe itself is God, then everything in the universe, including stones, trees, animals, and human beings, are parts of God and since all humans are capable of reason, all are endowed with logos. Of course, one could argue that if God is simply identical to Nature, this is only atheism by another name. However, Stoics would insist that the cosmos can rightly be called God because, according to them, the cosmos is intelligent. To be more precise, Stoics identify God as a universal mind or reason present in all things, and the physical cosmos is God's body. Though ancient Stoics emphasized the existence of God, this god was not personal. Hence, people are free to do or think what they want, because this god has no need of their praise or worship.[4]

Stoics believe that the laws of nature are good evidence that the world was designed with purpose, and claim that humans' ability to reason suggests that we are created by something that also possesses reason. Cicero, in his work *On the Nature of the Gods,* attributes the following argument to Zeno. "Nothing without a share in mind and reason can give birth to one who is animate and rational. But the world gives birth to those who are animate and rational. Therefore, the world is animate and rational" (2.22).

According to the Roman Stoic philosopher Epictetus, humans were created by the god Zeus (by which he probably meant Nature). Epictetus explained that Zeus made human being different from other animals by giving them rationality, a condition they shared with the gods. As a result, humans are a curious hybrid, part animal and part god. Epictetus, like Seneca before him, argued that God, like an effective coach or physical trainer, tests and hardens us by life's adversities "for his own service," and for our own benefit and improvement.

Following the presocratic philosopher Heraclitus, Stoics claim that the world is organized by reason (*logos* in Greek). Heraclitus said, "all things come to pass in accordance with this Word [*logos*]" (Fragment 2). *Logos,* a complicated term, has many meanings; it can mean "reason," "argument," even "speech" or "word." As previously noted, some modern classicist scholars claim that the Stoic conception of *logos* likely influenced the author of

---

4. On the surface, this view has many parallels with the theological perspective called panentheism, a view discussed in chapter 3 and favored by many contemporary Christians.

the gospel of John, which begins, "In the beginning was the Word [*logos*], and the *logos* was with God, and the *logos* was God" (John 1:1).

To highlight the importance of theology, Zeno's successors accorded it a prominent position in its own right. Cleanthes explicitly set off theology from the rest of physics, and wrote a separate volume On the Gods. Likewise, Chrysippus published works *On the Gods* and *On Zeus*, placing physics at the final stage of the curriculum and the study of theology as the final and climactic topic to be taught, making it the proper object of study for the advanced student of philosophy and likely only for the virtuous, that is, the wise. In this respect physics, including theology, followed the study of logic and ethics, bringing the study of philosophy to a close. Whereas Stoic theology came to be regarded as the culmination of the philosophical curriculum, in Christianity theology was given primacy, becoming the source or basis for ethics and physics.

Despite their apparent belief in God, Stoics claim to be materialists, for they view the soul and the universal mind present in all things to be made of matter, although of a rarified and noble kind of matter. This means that, unlike the God of the Abrahamic traditions, the Stoic God is not omnipotent. His power is limited by natural and logical possibility. These limitations, at least in part, explain why there is evil in the world. Chrysippus, one of Zeno's immediate successors, taught that the existence of good and evil were interdependent. As it is logically impossible for good to exist without evil, so God designed a world that makes the best of this situation. Thus, evil may exist at the local level, but it is used by God to perfect the whole.

Once again following Heraclitus, the Stoics believe that reality is in flux. Everything is constantly changing. To the Stoics, all things unfold according to the rational plan of God. Thus, Stoics are strict determinists. Time unfolds exactly according to God's plan, and the history of the cosmos repeats eternally. Everything began in a conglomeration of fire, everything will collapse back into it, and eventually the cosmos will begin again unfolding exactly as it always has. There is no reason for future world cycles to change, because God's plan for the cosmos is as good as it could possibly be.

In the Stoic cosmos, everything is fully determined. There is, in their view, a cause for every event in the cosmos. Despite believing in a deterministic universe, ruled by divine fate, Stoics do not deny human freedom. Thus, they are compatibilists, believing that fate and free will are compatible. Stoics claim that our decisions and attitudes are up to us, and even though they are determined by causes, they are our choices. It is with our intellect that we decide to do what we do. We are not constrained from doing anything against our will, which is consistent with causal determinism. And because everything unfolds according to God's plan, we should embrace our fate.

As we have seen, the Stoic God is not a transcendent omniscient being standing outside nature, but rather is wholly immanent—the divine element being immersed in nature itself. What is important to Stoics is their belief that the universe is ruled by a just law. This means, everything follows a rational and logical order. Therefore, all things follow the same rules and laws, and no matter how hard we fight to bend or break them, they will endure.

One clear distinction between traditional Stoics and Christians is the former's reliance on logic and reason, as opposed to the latter's reliance on faith and revelation. Whereas in the past, Stoicism was a personal religion designed to create a form of spirituality that raised people's souls toward the cosmic God, that emphasis does not characterize all modern Stoics. While traditional Stoics believed in a pantheistic god of sorts—also described as the Universal Reason, Divine Nature, or Logos—modern Stoics do not consider the existence or lack of a god or deity central to their beliefs, since many consider themselves agnostics or atheists. Whereas modern Christians, following their enlightenment predecessors, claim allegiance to some form of theism, most also value the use of science and reason. An increasing minority, however, following a mystical and nondualist persuasion, are coming to value the apophatic path of unknowing as the best and perhaps only way of knowing ultimate reality.

Questions for Discussion and Reflection

Select one or more of the following questions and write your answer(s) in a journal. If you are in a group study, be prepared to share your answers with those in the group.

1. Stoics are often viewed as going through life while attempting to suppress their emotions. Why is this wrong?
2. Explain what Stoics mean by *eudaimonia* and a eudaimonic life.
3. Explain the core concept underlying virtue-based philosophy. In your estimation, does Christianity qualify as such a philosophy? Explain your answer.

4. Using the "archer metaphor," explain and assess the role of "indifference" in Stoicism.
5. What do Stoics mean by "living according to nature"?
6. What do Stoics mean by "the dichotomy of control"?
7. Of the seven Stoic attitudes toward life, which do you consider most important and which least important? Explain your answer.
8. Explain the similarities and differences between Stoic views of God and the perspective called panentheism.
9. Stoics believe that the only true evil is ignorance. In your estimation, what does this mean, and how does it underscore the role of "logic" in classic Stoic pedagogy?
10. By combining human freedom with cosmic determinism, Stoics are said to be compatibilists. Assess the validity of this position and its affinity with your own thinking on this topic.
11. After reading this chapter, what aspect, teaching, or quality of Stoicism do you find most attractive or compelling and which least compelling? Explain your answer.

12

Role Ethics in Stoicism and Christianity

THE STOIC BELIEF SYSTEM rests on three essential beliefs: (1) that virtue is sufficient for happiness, (2) that other so-called goods should be regarded with indifference, and (3) that the world is providentially ordered by God. Through its essential beliefs and attitudes, Stoicism has had a lasting impact on the history of thought. It influenced the development of Christian morality and theology, but also modern philosophy. While early church theologians regarded Stoicism as a "pagan philosophy" rather than as a personal religion, nonetheless, early Christian writers employed central philosophical concepts of Stoicism such as "Logos," "virtue," "Spirit," and "conscience."

Another affinity between Stoicism and Christianity is the concept of "role ethics," a significant feature in both systems or ways of life. According to role ethics, each human being is a member of the human cosmopolis, that is, a citizen of the global community. Ultimately, all human beings need to work in concert to make sure they provide a better present for all and a better future for coming generations. The basic idea behind role ethics is that every individual plays a variety of roles in life—father, son, mother, daughter, boss, employee, and so forth—and that a life worth living involves balancing those roles in the most harmonious way possible.

According to the ancient Stoic philosopher Epictetus, there are fundamentally three kinds of roles: our basic role a human beings and members of human society; roles that are given to us by circumstances, such as being someone's daughter or son; and roles that we choose for ourselves, such as by getting married, having children, or being someone's friend. Stoics consider our role as members of human society the most important. Within that overarching guideline, we all need to balance our specific roles the best way possible. Such a goal requires compromise. When we contemplate the competing demands of our professional and family lives, we are forced to consider if and how much compromise we must make, and for this we go to the cardinal virtues for guidance. In his *Enchiridion*, a practical manual to life the eudaimonic life, Epictetus noted that when human beings set out to do something, they should keep two goals in mind; first, they must seek to remain in harmony with nature,[1] and second, they need to distinguish what things are within their power and what things are not. The only thing within our power are our judgments, our motivation, and what we consciously pursue or avoid. These three categories correspond to Epictetus's three disciplines: assent, action, and desire. Taken together, they emphasize that we should act reasonably and pro-socially.

To understand role ethics, it is helpful to examine the Stoic notion of cosmopolitanism, articulated initially by the Stoic Musonius Rufus, who lived in Rome during the first century CE, and later developed more fully a century later by his pupil and influential author Hierocles. Musonius was a follower of the Stoic Roman nobleman Gaius Plautus, who was a rival of the emperor Nero. When Nero exiled his rival in the year 60, Musonius followed his friend out of loyalty as well as dislike for the emperor's tyrannical ways. Both Plautus and Musonius were part of the Stoic opposition, a group of senators and philosophers who dared to criticize Nero and two of his successors, Vespasian and Domitian.

When Nero had Plautus executed in the year 62, Musonius returned to Rome. Accused of participating in a failed conspiracy against the emperor, Musonius was exiled to the rugged Greek island of Gyranos, where he created a small philosophical community. Musonius returned to Rome

---

1. When ancient Greeks spoke of nature, they had in mind not what conditions are or have been, but what they can become under the most favorable conditions. While modern individuals connect the term with the origin of something, ancient philosophers connected it with the end, goal, or *telos* of something. Thinking along these lines, when the author of Matthew exhorts the followers of Jesus to "be perfect," as God is perfect (Matt 5:48), he has in mind fulfilling or living out one's natural potential. By "nature," then, Stoics and other ancient philosophers had in mind the highest and best of civilization. Hence, when Aristotle maintained that the State is a natural product, it is because it evolved out of social relations that exist naturally. Following this conception, ancient Stoics viewed a person's natural life as a life lived in accordance with its highest perfection or ideal. As rational beings, humans should cultivate the rational life. And for ancient philosophers, the perfection of reason was the ultimate virtue. For this reason, the ways of nature are none other than the ways of virtue.

in 68, during the rule of the emperor Vespasian, where he embarked on his teaching career, including his most famous student, Epictetus, who later became one of the most celebrated of all Stoics. Considered a political nuisance, Musonius was exiled again in the year 71, returning some eight years later after Vespasian's death. While not much of Musonius's legacy remains, we do have a collection of lectures and sayings put together by a student named Lucius.

From his lectures we learn that Musonius disagreed with academic philosophers in general, viewing them as simple technicians rather than as role models. While he did not discard the value of theoretical learning, he built on Socrates's argument that virtue is a skill that can be taught. For Musonius, our goal as human is to become better persons, something one learns from good philosophers.

In his third lecture, Musonius makes a surprising feminist point for his time, though many Stoics have echoed it since Zeno had stated it nearly four hundred years earlier, namely, that women are equal with men, and should have similar upbringing and education. In his estimation, there was only one type of virtue, and it applied equally for men and women: "Just as no man would be properly educated without philosophy, so no woman would be either." Such philosophical teaching requires practice, for "the person who wants to be good must not only learn the lessons that pertain to virtue but train themselves to follow them eagerly and rigorously." Becoming adept at life, like training in any sport, art, or profession, requires training. For example, a philosopher can explain what temperance is in such a way that we would know what it means, but learning alone won't make you a temperate person.

In his eighteenth lecture he provides a good example of how such practice might go. There he speaks of mastering one's appetite for food and drink, finding such mastery to be the beginning and basis for self-control. Thus, if one wants to become more temperate, one can start with one's eating habits, for the failure to control one's eating and drinking habits correlates directly with one's physical, mental, emotional, and spiritual health. Hence, for Musonius, temperance is the beginning of—and basis for—self-control. In order to gain self-control, he provides some mental guidance. For example, don't think you are depriving yourself by not reaching for another glass of wine or a third helping of the main dish. Instead, remind yourself that you are improving your character—that by not following your physical urges you are actually engaging in something positive for yourself.

To grow in discipline, he advises, reframe your therapy as a challenge rather than as a sacrifice. And be forgiving of yourself when you inevitably slip. After all, we are human beings, but not all of us are saints or sages.

While only a few lectures of Musonius remain, only several hundred lines of text remain from Hierocles's most important work, *Elements of Ethics*. Nevertheless, despite the paucity of sources, Hierocles is famous for his rendition of two fundamental and highly interconnected classic Stoic concepts: *oikeiosis* or sense of belonging, and cosmopolitanism. *Oikeiosis* denotes a process that begins at birth and continues throughout life. It begins as something instinctual, but over time, practicing it is a deliberate choice that humans make as rational beings. While the instinct of all animals, humans included, is to protect themselves and look after their immediate interests, in social species, humans recognize the need to develop a concern for those who immediately surround them, especially their caretakers. This, then, is the first step of the oikeiotic process, expanding from "me" to "us." As we recognize from the teaching of Jesus known as the Golden Rule, this process recognizes the value and fairness of treating others kindly and fairly, as we would like them to treat us.

While *oikeiosis* describes this process of expanding circles of concern, the outermost circle is the entire human race. And that brings us to the Stoic concept of cosmopolitanism. Despite being inherent in many philosophies and religions, the concept of cosmopolitanism still has not won the day, particularly in the West, where individualistic, consumeristic, and capitalistic values reign. And yet this is the only way forward, the only way to end poverty and war, sustain our natural environment, and build a better future for everyone. According to cosmopolitanism—a vision Stoicism shares with Christianity and philosophy with theology—we humans will only be able to overcome our superficial differences when we focus on our shared humanity, something we can only accomplish by "loving God and our neighbor as ourself."

Classic Stoic Role Models

The ancient Stoics used role models to improve their character. They recognized that people can fool themselves into justifying a particular course of action that might be more convenient than ethical. We can counter this natural tendency to stray by choosing role models whose characters we can emulate. They came up with a list of real and fictional role models whose virtues they used to guide their personal growth and self-development. One of the most famous of these was Cato the Younger, one of the most respected politicians and generals of the late Roman Republic. In the first century BCE, Rome had fallen under the control of a dictator named Sulla, who gained control of Rome after a bloody civil war. Sulla began a series of reprisals against his political enemies, killing scores of them and enriching himself and his friends with the profits from the sale of their properties. As a teenager, Cato was often a guest of the dictator and witnessed some of these atrocities in person.

One day Cato asked his tutor why nobody got rid of the tyrant, and his tutor replied that people were afraid to take action. Later, as an adult politician and revenue official in the territory of Cyprus, Cato refused to engage in the usual corrupt and self-enriching behavior of Roman administrators. Eventually, in opposition to what he perceived as the tyranny of the Roman dictator Julius Caesar, Cato joined Pompey the Great's republican army against Caesar. In 48 BCE, after Caesar defeated Pompey, Cato collected the remainder of the rebel army and made a last stand at Utica, in modern-day Tunisia. Caesar made it clear that he wanted Cato captured alive so that he could use him as a political pawn, but Cato had different intentions.

After a final dinner and conversation with his family and friends, he retired to his room to read Plato's *Phaedo*, which recounts the last hours of Socrates's life, whereupon he stabbed himself to death. The story of how Cato died was often mentioned by the first-century Stoic philosopher Seneca as the quintessential example of Stoic virtue and courage. Centuries later, Dante gave Cato a prime role in his narrative poem *The Divine Comedy*, having the Stoic stand guard at the entrance of the Mountain of Purgatory. As the poet put it, "What man on earth was more worthy to signify God than Cato? Surely none." While the idea of a Stoic role model isn't that one needs to be ready to imitate Cato, the focus is for us to think or ordinary and extraordinary people we admire and upon whose values and behavior we might pattern our own.

Not all Stoic role models were living people; some were imaginary, mythological figures. One was Odysseus—or Ulysses, as the Romans called him—the Homeric hero who captured Troy with his famous wooden horse and then spent ten years making his way home to his wife and son, with all sorts of obstacles thrown his way by the angry god Poseidon. Odysseus embodied a major tenet of Stoicism in the obligation to accept his fate. He was a role model for the Stoics because he was committed to playing his roles in life while at the same time not confusing such roles with who he truly was. He was the king of Ithaca, a warrior on the planes of Troy, the captain of his ship during the voyage home, a faithful husband to Penelope, and an inspiring father to his son Telemachus. However, he also seems to have had a moral purpose that transcended his individual roles: he was steadfast, loyal, determined, and courageous. Epictetus used Odysseus to illustrate the notion of cosmopolitanism. To be virtuous, we don't have to spend all of our lives in a single place. Learning and respecting other people's ways is an important path for intellectual, psychological, and spiritual growth.

Jesus of Nazareth as Mentor and Role Model

In addition to ancient role models such as Socrates, whose death at the hands of the state made him the first martyr to the cause of wisdom, we must add Jesus of Nazareth, the rustic Galilean sage who was crucified for threatening the religious and political authorities of his day with the claim that his kingdom was not of this world. A role model for all Christians, not only in death but in life, he is revered not only as the second member of the Trinity but perhaps more so for modeling servanthood by being wholly human. The early Christians began with a view of Jesus that was uncomplicated and relatable. They certainly did not see Jesus to be of *merely* human significance but as one who embodied what God was doing in their midst.

According to many Christians, the death of Jesus was the purpose of his life on earth and was central to God's plan for humanity. In their view, Jesus knew in advance the details of his death and viewed them as central to his messianic vocation and purpose in life. However, in the judgment of many biblical scholars, this understanding of the life and death of Jesus, often labeled "atonement theology," is not biblical and does not go back to Jesus. Rather, it was formulated in the Middle Ages by Anselm of Canterbury (1033–1109), who defined the doctrine of atonement that became normative in the West: God became man in order to expiate the sin of Adam.

While atonement theology is central to evangelical preaching and teaching, it erroneously compresses the overarching storyline of the Bible into a conversionist template. While the concept of salvation, fully understood, is essential to biblical theology, the starting point to this concept is not the death of Jesus, but rather his life. It is not Jesus' death, but rather his life that is central to God's plan for humanity. Jesus came, not to die, but

Christlikeness

to live, and through his life and teachings to illustrate and illuminate the meaning of human life.

After having stood at the center of Christianity for two thousand years, in recent times Jesus has been made the poster boy for all sorts of causes, from middle-class moralist to enlightened guru, from hellfire preacher to social justice warrior—and the list grows every year. The reason Jesus keeps getting a rebrand—the reason his image simple refuses to go away—is that he is without question the most influential person in history.

As the central character in the Bible, the world's best-selling book, Jesus is known the world over. In addition to being the central figure in Christianity, Jesus is also a significant figure in Islam, where he is revered as prophet. Despite having been rejected by Jews as Messiah, Jesus remains the most famous Jew of all time. Furthermore, he is admired the world over as martyr, saint, and mentor, his character revered by Hindus, Buddhists, Daoists, and Shintos alike.

Staggering inequality exists around the world today, a phenomenon that goes back into remote antiquity, when it seemed quite normal to treat people unequally. Most ancient civilizations practiced slavery, a practice defended by philosophical idealists and realists such as Plato and Aristotle. In addition, slavery, caste systems, child marriages, and honor killings continue to be tragically commonplace, perpetuated culturally as deeply held beliefs. Thankfully, such practices are countered by the ideals of equality, a mindset emphasized by Jesus and perpetuated in western cultures by Jesus-inspired followers.

By his embrace of women, children, the poor, outsiders, and other people marginalized by society, and through teachings such as his claim that God knows the number of hairs on our head and his call for shepherds to leave the ninety-nine for the one who is lost, Jesus defied the ancient world to insist that every life matters. In teaching that all people are created equal, Jesus forever offers a better way to cultural superiority and ideologies based on sexism, racism, and classism.

Because of Jesus, our definition of hero has changed. In antiquity, heroes were deeply flawed humans. Most, such as conquering emperors, samurai warriors, and knights in bright armor, were violent and necessarily partisan. On the contrary, many today esteem people who serve the needy, rescuers who sacrifice their lives for others, and leaders who relate to the humble and lowly. Once again, this extraordinary reversal is attributable to Jesus, who washed his disciples' dirty feet, who articulated claims such as the meek will inherit the earth, and who gave up his life for his friends.

Through his example, it may be said that Jesus paved the way for democracy, a form of government adopted by some 70 percent of the world's nations. Underlying democracy is the rule of law, the idea that a nation is governed by its constitution—something with higher authority than that of monarchs, presidents, senators, or mob majority. For this, followers of Jesus were inspired by the scriptures and laws of ancient Israel, which in turn were central in drafting foundation texts of modern democracy such as the Magna Carta, the English Bill of Rights, and the U.S. Declaration of Independence. These documents reasoned that if all human beings are made in God's image, a nation's citizens and not simply its elite should determine how government is formed and maintained, including responsibility to institute checks and balances to restrain its corruption. These revolutionary ideas, including human rights such as freedom of speech, press, assembly, and religion, have deeply Christian roots.

Based on the example of Jesus, his early followers proceeded to turn the world upside down, beginning with the imperial city of Rome. While early Christians were despised in the Roman Empire, their programs to feed Rome's poor rivaled the city's civic guilds. Christians also scoured streets and trash heaps to rescue discarded babies—their example ultimately ending infanticide.

Christianity and compassion are deeply linked. Public healthcare, unknown in the ancient world, is largely due to the efforts of Jesus' disciples such as the Cappadocian church father Basil of Caesarea (330–379), who opened a 300-bed hospital in Cappadocia around 372. His vision gradually took hold, until medieval monks were caring for the sick in 37,000 European monasteries. As modern medicine was born, followers of Jesus led the charge again, pioneering antiseptic surgery, clinical teaching, physiology, transplant surgery, vaccines, and care for patients with contagious diseases.

The world wouldn't be the same without Christian heroes like William Carey, who ended widow burning in India; William Wilberforce, who abolished the slave trade; the British humanitarian Lord Shaftsbury, who helped abolish child labor, women working in coal mines, and treating the insane with cruelty; Martin Luther King Jr., who transformed civil rights in the U. S.; Nelson Mandela, who after twenty-seven years in prison, took the path of understanding and reconciliation to help overthrow the apartheid government of South Africa, ultimately becoming his country's first Black

Christlikeness

president; and Mother Teresa, whose name is a synonym for compassion. While Christians have no monopoly on care, it was Jesus—who gave us the parable of the Good Samaritan and backed it up with his profound love for the hungry, sick, and dying—who inspired more compassion than any single person, movement, or force in history.

Points of Compatibility between Christianity and Stoicism

While one could simply dismiss the topic of compatibility between Christianity and Stoicism by labeling the former a religion and the latter a philosophy, can we simply set aside much of the theological baggage that developed over the centuries and go back to the ethical teachings and way of life modeled by Jesus, Paul, and the apostles, as well as by Socrates, Seneca, and their philosophical pupils, who came, not to start a new religion, but to live a fully human life, based upon the premise that all humans, sharing God's image, deserve to be loved, respected, and treated with kindness and compassion.

Among the points of compatibility between these two ways of life, the following are significant:

1. The Stoic view of God is harmonizable with a Christian panentheistic view of God. Stoics believe that everything in this world is an interrelated part of a great whole. They believe in a just law that runs the universe, and that all things exists to support and benefit the greater good. Stoics, like Christians, would insist that the cosmos is intelligent; to be more precise, they identify God as a universal mind or reason present in all things. They also believe that the laws of nature are good evidence that the world was designed with purpose, and claim that human being are created by something that possesses reason. While Stoics adhere to the principle that the world is organized by reason or Logos, unlike traditional Christian theology, the Stoic God is not a transcendent omniscient being standing outside nature, but rather is immersed in nature itself. Affirming the concept of providence, they believe in a just law that runs the universe. However, unlike traditional Christians, Stoics do not trust in beliefs, but rather in holistic living. Hence, rather than worship a sovereign being, either out of love or fear, they are free to do or think what they want, because their God has no need of praise or worship. Instead, they tend to be happy people

who are content with their lives, and who emphasize that by living virtuously, they serve the will of the Logos/God.

2. The Stoics' greatest legacy is their ethics, and their ethical goal—to attain inner peace by overcoming adversity, practicing self-control, realizing our ephemeral nature and the short time allotted to one's life—includes meditative practices that also help Christians live in harmony with nature and not against it. In antiquity, philosophy was perceived as the art of life. The goal of the philosopher from Socrates onward was to practice and teach this art to others. Stoicism and Christianity both enjoin people to overcome unwholesome desires and to pursue virtue. In the New Testament, the influence of Stoic philosophy is particularly evident in the letter of James. There, the primary role of the leader of the church is the sage or teacher, whose primarily aim is to develop wisdom (3:1–7). The good works produced by wisdom include such standard Stoic virtues as steadfastness and endurance (1:2–4) and the call to seriousness of purpose, to recognize the beneficence of God, and to live in accord with the perfect law (1:5–25). Questions of leadership roles or rank within the community are never discussed, for James's model, like the stoic model of leadership, is egalitarian.

3. Stoics, like most Christians, are guided by role ethics, and while Stoics use philosophical role model to guide their lives and behavior, Christians are guided by the life and teachings of Jesus, specifically the Golden Rule and the Great Commandment to love God and others as extensions of oneself. Like Jesus, Stoic teachers remind their followers not to get attached to their possessions. Life is transitory, and one should live and enjoy each day fully, as a gift from God. For Stoics and Christians alike, individual happiness is primarily determined by the condition of one's soul, rather than by the conditions of one's body, status, or possessions.

4. Unlike Stoics, who are inclusive, Christians have been known to live and think exclusively. In so doing, however, they counter the ideals and practices of Jesus, who affirmed the values of cosmopolitanism by emphasizing the unity, equality, and oneness of all human beings, and who treated all living creatures with compassion and respect.

5. For Stoics, the identification of God with both providence and fate involved the need to redefine the relation between God and humanity as traditionally conceived, in particular the way in which God

Christlikeness

communicates to human (divination) and humans communicate to God (prayer). Epicurus ridiculed the idea of a theistically conceived God waiting for the promptings of humans in order to take appropriate action. While emphasizing the value of traditional religion over impiety, Stoics avoid prayer and similar incongruities by emphasizing divination, in a pantheistic rather than a theistic way, as not involving any specific and intentional course of action on the part of God but as something made possible by the providentially ordered sequence of causes and effects in the cosmos. While some Stoics seemed to make room for the practice of prayer as efficacious, primarily as a form of meditation or self-address, namely, as a means of ensuring that one's internal daimon be in tune with cosmic virtue or rationality, none viewed it as efficacious in currying favor with God or as a means of persuading or changing God's will. Rather, ancient Stoics preferred divination, viewing it as a science harmonious with the ways of a deterministic universe. According to Seneca, Stoics do not honor God/the gods by sacrificial offering but by right and virtuous intentions; God seeks no servants, and the proper worship of God is to live virtuously.

6. Jesus, like most ancient Stoics, was a nondualist, for he had a unified view of reality. Stoics also provided a unified account of reality, constructed from ideals of logic, monistic physics, and naturalistic ethics. As monistic materialists, Stoics view all reality as composed of one or more of the four natural (material) elements: earth, air, fire, and water. Following Heraclitus, who declared fire as the universal First Cause and therefore likened God/the world to an ever-living Fire, most Stoics view fire as the most powerful of the elements, for they see fire both as the strongest source of power and energy in the universe and as the embodiment of the gods. While the Christian scriptures view God as Spirit (John 4:24), they too speak of God as fire (see Heb 12:29; also Deut 4:24; Exod 3:2; 13:21). Cleanthes, wishing to give explicit meaning to Zeno's "creative fire," seems to have been the first to use the term *pneuma* or "spirit" to describe the First Cause. Like fire, this intelligent "Spirit" was imagined as a tenuous substance akin to air or breath, but essentially possessing the quality of warmth. Stoics viewed this life-giving spirit (*pneuma*) immanent in the universe as God, present in inert objects as a state or disposition (*hexis*), in plants as nature (*phusis*), in animals as soul (*psychē*), and in human being as mind or reason (*logos*). Clearly, it is a short

step from this to the Holy Spirit of Christian theology. The apostle Paul, who met with Stoics during his stay in Athens, often used Stoic terms and metaphors to assist Gentile converts in their understanding of Christianity (see, for example, Acts 17:28).

7. Stoics, like Christians, contributed the element of hope to the topic of eschatology. While Christians were confident that victory over evil had begun when God raised Jesus from the dead, Stoics philosophers such as Seneca affirmed in his treatise *On Providence* the divine order of the universe and how history would culminate in the renewal of the universe, at which time the souls of the blest would share in peace and immortality. In competing for adherents, however, Christianity had a major advantage over Stoicism, for it promised not just life after death but an afterlife in which one would be infinitely satisfied for an eternity. Stoics, on the other hand, thought it possible that there was life after death, but they were not certain of it, and if there was life after death, they were uncertain what it would be like. The Stoic philosopher and emperor Marcus Aurelius, while affirming the beneficence of Providence, was keenly aware of human sin and wickedness. In this life, he longed for freedom, but he expected to find it only beyond death.

8. Finally, Stoics and Christians alike believe in the creator's plans and purpose behind everything. Like Christianity, Stoicism claimed that the gods created human beings, cared about their well-being, and gave them a divine element (the ability to reason). Christianity claimed that God created us, cares about us personally, ang gave us a divine element (a soul). Thus, both systems exhort us to love and respect nature and all living creatures as God's body. While ancient Stoics were pantheists and materialists and ancient Christians were monotheists and spiritualist, both came to understand the limits of the human mind and to value the mystery and unknowability of ultimate reality.

Questions for Discussion and Reflection

Select one or more of the following questions and write your answer(s) in a journal. If you are in a group study, be prepared to share your answers with those in the group.

1. After reading this chapter, what did you learn about "role ethics"?

Christlikeness

2. Role ethics is said to differ fundamentally from "standard ethics." Explain the difference between these ethical approaches.

3. Stoics believe that when we set out to do something, we should keep two goals in mind. What are they?

4. The traditional Stoic curriculum included the study of physics, logic, and ethics. What do Stoics mean by "ethics"? What do they mean by "physics"?

5. Explain the Stoic concept of cosmopolitanism.

6. After reading this chapter, what did you learn about becoming a temperate person?

7. What trait do classic Stoic role models have in common?

8. After reading this chapter, what did you learn about following Jesus as role model?

9. In addition to Jesus or his apostles, what person or persons do you uphold as essential role models in your life? Explain your answer.

10. After reading this chapter, what Stoic feature or factors do you find most attractive or compelling, and which least compelling? Explain your answer.

11. In your estimation, is a synthesis between Stoicism and Christianity desirable or possible? If so, which beliefs or practices must Stoicism be willing to set aside, and which must Christians be willing to set aside?

13

The Theological Virtues

WHILE CHRISTIANS AGREE WITH the Western philosophic tradition on the importance of virtue, and of the four virtues in particular, they disagree with non-Christian philosophy in their understanding of how the moral life starts and on the severity of the obstacles. There seems to be an impediment at work in our lives that draws us away from the habits of virtue and makes it difficult to act on them. For Christianity, what stands between us and virtue is sin. Sin is much more serious than the simple fact that we often fail to do the things we know we ought to do. Sin is spiritual nearsightedness, a constriction at the center of human life that keeps us turned in upon ourselves, so that we cannot live as God intends. The good news that Christianity proclaims is that God has provided the resources to overcome our moral myopia, expanding our vision by showing us in Jesus what life is like when it is lived in love for God and for other people.

In addition to the moral virtues, there must be characteristic changes in human life that mark the turn from self to God, from limited human resources to divine resources; and these, according to Christianity, are God's gifts, not human achievements. In addition to those cardinal virtues that enable us to learn and maintain the other moral virtues, there must be supernatural virtues, "habits of choice and action that guide us in seeing our lives in relation to God and help us to persevere in that orientation, even when it is not immediately supported by our experience or by people around us."[1]

---

1. Lovin, *Christian Ethics*, 76.

Christlikeness

For Christian writers like Thomas Aquinas, the supernatural virtues were conveniently summarized in the three abiding realities mentioned in 1 Corinthians 13: faith, hope, and love. Like the cardinal virtues, the theological virtues are "hinges" on which the good life turns. Without them all other virtues are unsteady. Without faith, hope, and love, patience and kindness are apt to wilt under stress or, worse, be transformed into manipulative ways to serve oneself under the guise of helping others. Temperance, courage, prudence, and justice make us more effective in the application of moral virtues, but not if our pursuit of goodness is directed, in the end, toward our own gain. What Christian morality requires is a reorientation of our life whereby the theological virtues become central to how we live and to how we relate with other people, and not simply instrumental to our own self-improvement.

Speaking theologically, every power we have is given by God. Like other spiritual qualities, the theological virtues are paradoxical in that they are *gifts* that cannot be obtained by merely wishing for them, but they are also *virtues* that can be cultivated. While their potential is available to all persons alike, the capacity for faith, hope, and love varies with one's constitution and one's social circumstances. Faith is called "the seed," for without it the plant of spiritual life cannot start at all. In fact, so fundamental is faith that none of us can live well for long without it. This is true of all religions, and even the pseudo-religions of modern times such as Socialism, Secularism, and Scientism.

To be effective, four factors go into the transformation process that occurs when supernatural gifts become central in our lives:

1. *Intellectual*: our minds must be renewed. This is what Paul proposed when he exhorted his readers: "Do not be conformed to this world [and its ways of thinking], but be transformed by the renewing of your minds, so that you may discern what is the will of God—what is good and acceptable and perfect" (Rom 12:2).

2. *Volitional*: our wills must be renewed. All virtues involve the will, and like the other virtues, faith, hope, and love imply a resolute and courageous act of will. This emphasis combines the steadfast resolution that one *will* do something with the self-confidence that one *can* do it. The opposites of this are timidity, cowardice, fear, indecision, and a mean and calculating mentality. Paul exhorts his readers to exhibit this attitude, calling it the "mind of Christ": "Be of the same mind,

having the same love, being in full accord and of one mind. Do nothing from selfish ambition or conceit, but in humility regard others as better than yourselves. Let each of you look not to your own interests, but to the interests of others. Let the same mind be in you that was in Christ Jesus" (Phil 2:2–5).

3. *Emotional*: our hearts must be renewed. In practicing the virtues, our attitude should be serene and lucid, trusting in God and in God's care for us. This is what the first Evangelist, quoting Jesus, exhorts of his followers in the Sermon on the Mount: "Do not worry about your life, what you will eat or what you will drink, or about your body, what you will wear. Is not life more than food, and the body more than clothing? . . . . But strive first for the kingdom of God and his righteousness, and all these things will be given to you as well. So do not worry about tomorrow, for tomorrow will bring worries of its own. Today's trouble is enough for today" (Matt 6:25, 33–34).

4. *Social*: our priorities and relationships must be renewed. When our state of being is submerged in cares about social circumstances, we become fixated in our own security and well-being, trusting in limited resources and relying on others to survive. When our faith turns from the visible and tangible to the invisible and elusive, our priorities become God's, and we become citizens of a different commonwealth, joining in the company of those who find strength out of weakness. As Paul reminds his readers: "[Christ's] grace is sufficient for you, for power is made perfect in weakness" (2 Cor 12:9). Behind faith, hope, and love stand the resources of the universe. As the author of the letter to the Hebrews famously defines faith: "Faith is the assurance of things hoped for, the conviction of things not seen" (Heb 11:1). It is with these invisible forces that one must learn to establish satisfactory social relations. In carrying out this task, the theological virtues require a considerable capacity for renunciation.

Faith

Viewed anthropologically, faith is a universal human concern, not necessarily religious in content or context. Faith can be an ordinary part of relationships in general, as in placing trust in someone or confidence in something. Faith helps us get in touch with the dynamic, patterned process by which we find life meaningful. Faith is a way of giving meaning to the forces and relations that make up our lives, how humans see themselves against a background of shared meaning and purpose. Prior to our being religious or irreligious, we are already engaged with putting our lives together and with what makes life worth living, looking for something to love that loves us, something to value that gives us value, something to honor and respect that has the power to sustain our being. These are issues of faith.

Viewed theologically, the reorientation of life to accommodate the centrality of the supernatural virtues begins with faith because we must trust that there is a reality beyond ourselves in which our goals find fulfillment and where our efforts finally make a difference. Without that reality there is no point to worrying about anything except in terms of how it makes our own life better. Without faith, personal success is the highest kind of goodness we can achieve. Religious faith may involve a leap, but such a leap, as physicist (and now Anglican priest) John Polkinghorne reminds us, is a "leap into the light, not the dark."[2] The aim of the religious quest, like that of the scientific quest, is to seek motivated belief about what is actually true. Faith should not be equated with shutting one's eyes or whistling in the dark.

Reasonable faith seeks understanding. Faith is an essential ingredient in making religious claims, but it does not work alone. Theologians use reason, not only to examine the grounds for religious claims, but also to understand them better. Faith may be a distinctive way to gain access to God, but it is not separable from other ways of knowing; in fact, it is a way of knowing. As modern scholarship has identified multiple forms of intelligence, so it recognizes multiple ways of knowing, involving eight human faculties: sense perception, reasoning, emotion, intuition, language, memory, imagination, and—significantly—faith. For some, faith is considered a deterrent to knowledge, because it does not rely on proof. For others, however, faith is the most important way to know, particularly that part of reality that eludes reason or the senses. Surely Blaise Pascal, the celebrated French physicist, mathematician, and philosopher, had faith in mind when he wrote, "The heart has reasons that reason cannot know."

---

2. Polkinghorne, *Quarks, Chaos, & Christianity*, 10.

The Theological Virtues

A Biblical Understanding of Faith

For the Bible, faith is the indispensable preliminary, without which true religious experience cannot develop. It involves a person's initial *awareness* of God, but also a continuing attitude of personal *trust* in God. The initiative is with God, but there must be the corresponding movement on the human side, and this is basically what is meant by faith. Religious and moral attainment is impossible without faith. As the New Testament affirms, all things are possible for the one who believes (Mark 9:23). And without faith, "it is impossible to please God (Heb 11:6).

In the Bible, faith is always relational, the object of faith being God, and the highest personalization is reached in the New Testament proclamation that God is best revealed in the life of Jesus. In this usage faith is a matter of personal relationship rather than abstract knowledge. In the Hebrew Bible the most important of the terms for faith is the root *amen*, meaning to trust someone. To say "Amen" to anyone is to trust that person, and in the Bible, nothing is as sure, permanent, or reliable as God.

Faith is essential to every religious, social, and political perspective, and it stands at the heart of Christianity. The concept is found throughout the New Testament, either as the noun "faith" (*pistis*) or the verb "believe" (*pisteuo*). When we examine the use of these words today, we discover that the common meaning of these words in modern English is very different from their premodern and ancient Christian meanings. When we speak of faith today, we usually have in mind "belief," which we take to mean holding a certain set of "beliefs," that is, "believing" certain doctrines or dogmas to be true. And that modern way of understanding "faith" leads to misreading key biblical texts. For instance, in the gospels, we often get the impression that Jesus insisted that his followers acknowledge his divine status, almost as a condition of discipleship. Those who beg him for healing are required to have faith before he can work a miracle, and one is commended for calling out: "I believe; help my unbelief" (Mark 9:24–25).

We do not find preoccupation with belief in the other major religious traditions, however, so we wonder, why did Jesus place such an emphasis on it? The answer is that he did not. The Greek word translated as "faith" in the New Testament means "trust, loyalty, or commitment." Jesus was not asking people to "believe" in his divinity, but rather was asking for commitment. He wanted disciples who would engage with his mission to abandon their pride, laying aside their self-importance and sense of entitlement, trusting fully in the God who was their father. In this freedom they were to give what they had to the poor, feed the hungry, and spread the good news of God's kingdom everywhere, living compassionate lives. Such *pistis* could move mountains and unleash human potential (Mark 11:22–23).

Faith and Hope Together

Hope is the inseparable companion of faith, the habit of acting on our faith. John Calvin spoke of hope as faith taken to the next level, calling hope "perseverance in faith." Faith gives us a reason to live; hope keeps us alive. Despair, hope's opposite, robs us of vitality, turning dreams into nightmares, vision into blindness. Faith, the foundation upon which hope rests, nourishes and sustains that faith. Apart from hope, faith becomes fainthearted and ultimately dead. Christian hope is nothing other than the expectation of those things that faith has believed to have been truly promised by God. Thus faith believes God to be true; hope awaits the time when this truth is made manifest. Faith believes that eternal life has been given to us; hope anticipates its manifestation. Faith binds us to Christ; hope opens this faith to the comprehensive future of Christ. In the Christian life "faith has the priority, but hope the primacy."[3] Thus it is that faith gives hope its assurance, but hope gives faith its breadth and its life.

Using an analogy from the physical body, faith and hope work together like our two lungs, or like the two hemispheres of our brain. As a pair of scissors is worthless without both blades working together, so faith and hope, working in tandem, help us actualize our God-given potential.

Believers whose lives and attitudes are characterized by faith and hope are sometimes viewed as naïve, because they trust in that which they cannot see and hope for things that seem unrealistic, or as Pollyannaish, because they always appear positive and upbeat. But my understanding of faith and hope is not limited to happy days or to good times. The only way people grow to be mature in their faith is to face their deepest fears and confront the greatest problems their society and world are facing and not lose hope.

At the beginning of my teaching career I recall confronting my parents with a list of personal fears and doomsday scenarios. My mother responded with the hope that fueled her faith in those times when her life was at risk as a missionary in Colombia—the Syria and Iraq of its day in the sense of violence, anarchy, and deep sectarian conflict—declaring that "the best is yet to come." My wife Susan, an effective pastoral counselor, asks her clients

3. Moltmann, *Theology of Hope*, 20.

to name the worst thing that can happen as a result of the situation they are facing. She understands that when persons are willing to confront their deepest fear, that that becomes their first step to victory. Faith and hope are inseparable, but they should never be confused with mere wish-fulfillment. They are most powerful when they are related to problems and threats in the real world.

Hope can sustain us through trials of faith, through human tragedies or difficulties that might seem overwhelming. In such circumstances, hope becomes an "anchor of the soul" (Heb 6:19). In the words of Pope Benedict XVI: "a distinguishing mark of Christians [is] the fact that they have a future."[4]

Hope

As Jürgen Moltmann reminds us in his book, *Theology of Hope*, when Christians contemplate the concept of hope, they are pondering the doctrine of eschatology, often defined as the "doctrine of last things," meaning speculation concerning the end of the world or what happens when one dies. As we see historically, apocalyptic theories abound during times of uncertainty, suffering, or persecution. At such times people ponder the future, conjuring utopian visions or issuing dire predictions. Unfortunately, the same holds true today, as apocalyptic cults, sects, even caliphates, flourish across the globe.

Whatever the word eschatology conjures in common speech, for Christians eschatology is a "doctrine of hope," for they are encouraged to live and think proleptically, that is, out of the resources of the future, as though the future were now. From first to last, Christianity is hope, forward looking and forward moving, and therefore also positively revolutionizing and transforming the present.

While speaking of the future, Christian eschatology is hopeful about the future, but it does not speak of the future as such. It sets out from a definite reality in history and announces the future of that reality, its future possibilities and its power over the future. Christian eschatology speaks of Jesus Christ and his future: Christ is our hope (Col 1:27). It recognizes the reality of the raising of Jesus and proclaims the future of the risen Lord. In thus announcing Christ's future in terms of promise, Christian eschatology

---

4. *Spe Salvi* ("In Hope We Are Saved," the papal encyclical letter dated November 30, 2007), §2.

points believers "toward the hope of [Christ's] still outstanding future. Hope's statements of promise anticipate the future. In the promises, the hidden future already announces itself and exerts its influence on the present through the hope it awakens."[5] Hope's statements of promise, therefore, do not result from experience, but are the condition for the possibility of new experiences. They do not seek to illuminate the reality which exists, but the reality that is coming.

Everywhere in the New Testament, the Christian hope is directed toward what is not yet visible: "Now hope that is seen is not hope" (Rom 8:24). Christian hope is resurrection hope, and it proves its truth in the contradiction of the future prospects it offers and guarantees: righteousness as opposed to sin, life as opposed to death, glory as opposed to suffering, peace as opposed to discord. Instead of portraying God as being wrathful and vengeful, as so many have done throughout history and are doing even today, it is vitally important to present hope as the foundation and the mainspring of theological thinking. That is why Jesus stands at the midpoint of history, reflecting God's true nature and pointing the way to a hopeful future. The question whether all statements about the future are grounded in the person and work of Jesus Christ provides the touchstone by which to distinguish the spirit of eschatology from that of utopia.

A Biblical Understanding of Hope

In English usage the word "hope" covers a wide range of meanings, and this holds true for the Bible as well. In both the Old and the New Testament the word "hope," whether as noun or as verb, points to a range of experience and meaning often missed in casual reading.

In the Hebrew Bible (Old Testament), hope sometimes describes a human condition of security and prosperity, in which individuals fear no threats and are confident that the future will sustain that security. However, in religious contexts, hope is defined not so much by the distinct shape of specific desires and expectations as by the fact that hope springs from God's creative and sustaining power and that it moves toward a good that is congruent with that power. Many images articulate the conviction that God alone provides the source and the object of our trust: God is a rock that cannot be moved, a refuge and fortress that offer ultimate security for the afflicted.

---

5. Moltmann, *Theology of Hope*, 17–18.

The Theological Virtues

Throughout the Old Testament, God is recognized as the "hope of Israel" (Jer 14:8). God's steadfast loving-kindness, revealed in repeated deeds of fidelity, gives the people of Israel confidence that God's promises will be fulfilled in the future. Thus God is the basis of all hope (Ps 33:18). Hope as a living, present bond between the God of hope and the hoping Israel becomes a major definition of the life of the righteous community. The response of the faithful is thus one of trust, through which one commits one's cause to God, holds fast to God, and lives in serenity and peace under God's protection. The confident expectation of future gladness leads to waiting in patience and courage.

False hope, namely hope in anyone or anything other than God, leads to chaos and disaster. Neither weapons of war, nor wealth, not idols can give lasting security. In the face of anticipated destruction, Jeremiah articulates the theme of the new covenant in classic words of hope: "I know the plans I have for you, says the Lord, plans for your welfare and not for harm, to give you a future with hope" (Jer 29:11).

Hope is a primary term in the New Testament. The word appears only as a noun or verb and never in adjectival or adverbial form, probably because the emphasis is not on subjective feeling (hopeful or hopefully) but on the objective nature of forces determining the human situation. For that reason the noun is never modified, as in "good" or "bad" hopes.

In the New Testament, hope occasionally describes a human expectation concerning the future that accords with a person's desires and expectations, but, as in the Old Testament, the emphasis is one's relationship with God. Here too hope is grounded in God, sustained by God, and directed by God. As such, hope is a reality within which humans may dwell. Hope is simultaneously the response by God's people to divine activity in their presence and on their behalf. If hope is fixed on God, hope embraces at once the three Hebrew elements of (1) expectation of the future, (2) trust, and (3) the patience of waiting. The connection of hope with faith in Hebrews 1:1 ("faith is the assurance of things hoped for") is quite in keeping with the Old Testament association of hoping and believing.

Paul's writings contain the most developed concept of hope in the New Testament. The famous triadic formula of "faith, hope, and love," noted in Paul's "love hymn" in 1 Corinthians 13, is found twice in 1 Thessalonians, Paul's earliest letter (1:3 and 5:8). Similarly, the three virtues are interrelated in Galatians 5:5–6, where hope, as a gift of the Holy Spirit, allows believers to actualize faith through love. In 1 Thessalonians 4:13, Paul warns his readers not to grieve, "as others do who have no hope" (cf. Eph 2:12), meaning not that they cannot imagine a future after death, but rather that they can have no well-founded trust in it. In 1 Corinthians 13:12–13, hope is not concerned with the realization of a human dream of the future, but with the confidence that waits patiently for God's gift.

Hope is one of the important components in Paul's dynamic understanding of faith. Strong faith and strong hope go together, as Paul indicates, using Abraham as an example in Romans 4:15–22. For Paul, hope emanates from faith, for hope reflects the guarantee that what God has begun in Christ will be brought to consummation (2 Cor 5:5). Hope is the linkage between what was begun in believers through their baptism and what will be completed at their resurrection (Rom 11:22; 1 Cor 15:2).

Romans 8:18–25 is an important text in that it shows that God's plan includes hope for the creation as well, which will share in freedom from decay and "obtain the glorious liberty of the children of God" (8:20).

Hope is a salient word in 1 Peter, which has been called the "letter of hope." In this epistle, hope has a present connotation. It is a "living hope," a mark of rebirth (1:3). The new life is participation in the resurrection of Jesus Christ. It is the eschatological gift that enables us to live as if the future is a present reality; therefore, hope is the power of this life. The source of our faith and the sustainer of our hope is God (1:21). Hope is the issue at stake in religious persecution; hope is to be confessed, defended, and explained on the witness stand. The defense that best conforms to this hope employs gentleness, courage, forgiveness, and reverence (3:13–17). As in Paul, the prime corollaries of hope are faith, joy, and love (1:3–9).

Love

In the beginning—love! Love is the act of will that at the beginning of time brought forth life. Love—God, energy, Being—is the primal force in the universe. Without love, nothing can exist. With love, all is possible.

Love, like faith and hope, is "the orientation of the individual life toward a center outside of itself, recognizing that my own value is not absolute, but derives from relationship to God. Love, likewise, values other people and things as they are related to God and not as they are useful or important to oneself. Love as a virtue, as a habit of choice and action, consistently does those things that enable others to flourish with their own

The Theological Virtues

dignity and their own relationship to God."[6] And that includes organizations, governments, and natural habitats under our care.

Having grown up during the 1960s, I remember Dionne Warwick singing the lyrics penned by Hal David, with music composed by Burt Bacharach: "What the world needs now is love, sweet love. It's the only thing that there's just too little of." Many singers recorded the song, its lyrics haunting and beautiful. I agree with the song's essential proposition, that we need to share more lavishly and compassionately this great resource called love, but is there too little love to go around, or only a misperception to that effect?

Actually, there is plenty of love on this planet, enough for all of us. The reason love seems to be lacking is because love is viewed as a distinct entity, somehow standing alone. If we had a supernatural understanding of love, we would understand that human love is insufficient on its own. It is only adequate for the needs of humanity when it is viewed as part of a triad, intrinsically bound to faith and hope. Like soul cannot survive without body and mind, love cannot thrive without faith and hope. So if we are rooted in faith and hope, we will have love as well.

According to the Bible, love is not something humans produce, or even earn. Love is everywhere, around us and within us, built into the cosmos by a loving Presence. As batteries in our phones and electronic devices need to be renewed regularly, so humans must immerse themselves in this original blessing, renewing their spirit by plugging regularly into God's boundless love, a resource present in every plant, flower, song, person, and situation. All we need to do is connect, absorb, enjoy, and share.

Love is the habit of choosing to be vulnerable by loving the good (what is right), and by acting accordingly. Love is like friendship; when we love our friends, we open ourselves to enjoy them for their own sake, and we wish good things for them. This is the attitude we should have toward creation, its creatures, and toward God. When we allow ourselves to be aware of and open to the goodness in the world, we are drawn to it and want to cherish it, and in this knowing and loving we are happy.

Love is not essentially about being nice or kind or generous; it is not primarily even about others, though such behavior follows. Love is primarily about our relationship with God. Speaking of love, Augustine called it "a movement of the soul toward enjoying God for God's own sake." Likewise Aquinas speaks of love as "friendship first with God and secondly with all

---

6. Lovin, *Christian Ethics*, 77.

who belong to God." Love, of course, naturally extends to authentic love of self, including our body, mind, personality, and emotions.

In a famous observation, Augustine argued that humanity is not merely created in the image of God, but rather in the image of the Trinity. He developed the idea of relationship within the members of the Trinity, claiming that the three persons are defined by their association to one another. Perhaps the most distinctive element of Augustine's approach was his use of the analogy of love, viewing the Father as the Lover, the Son as the Beloved, and the Spirit as the "bond of love" between the Father and the Son. In like manner, he saw the Spirit as the divine gift which binds believers to God. As the Holy Spirit is the love between the Father and the Son, love is the relationship between rational creatures and the world in which they find themselves. If we humans are the self-awareness of the cosmos, when we love nature and the mysterious cause of its existence we call God, we become like the Holy Spirit, and in this way, happy and fulfilled. We find here an amazing correlation: loving people are happy people; happy people are loving people. This is how we were meant to be.

A Biblical Understanding of Love

The concept of love in the Hebrew Bible (Old Testament) is used with reference to persons as well as actions and things, and there is a profane as well as a religious use. God's love is not depicted emotionally or intellectually but rather as a pointer to God's redeeming activity in human history; hence the focus of Israel's self-awareness on the notion of election, of being chosen. Love is a basic motif in God's dealings with Israel (Exod 15:13; Deut 4:37), an electing love always to a degree inexplicable. The bottom line seems to be: "God loves you" (Deut 7:8). In like manner, God also loves the victims of society, such as the orphan, the widow, and the sojourner (Deut 10:18–19).

The concept of God's steadfast love is depicted clearly in the prophetic literature, particularly by Hosea but also by Isaiah and Jeremiah. In Jeremiah 31:3, God is said to love Israel with an eternal love, and this love is the basis of God's faithfulness. Hosea reminds us that God desires relationship rather than ritual, intimacy rather than mundane worship: "For I desire steadfast love and not sacrifice, the knowledge of God rather than burnt offerings" (Hos 6:6).

In the Psalms, Israel hopes in God's love because God is known to be a loving God (Ps 147:11), watching over those who hope in his love (Ps

The Theological Virtues

33:18, 22). The expectation of ultimate salvation is the hope in God's covenantal love. God will save because of God's love (Ps 6:4; 33:26). Indeed, God's salvation and God's love can be spoken of as synonymous (Ps 85:7; 119:41; 130:7).

The Old Testament idea of the love of God is decisive for the New Testament idea of love. In Mark a Jewish scribe approaches Jesus and asks, "Which commandment is the first of all?" And Jesus answers by quoting from Deuteronomy 6:5 and Leviticus 19:8: "You shall love the Lord your God with all your heart, and with all your soul, and with all your mind, and with all your strength . . . and your neighbor as yourself" (Mark 12:29-31).

As this passage makes clear, God expects total response and commitment from those who claim to love God, even to the point of loving one's enemies (Matt 5:43-46). This love, which Jesus demands, is to characterize the new people of God, to whom the future belongs. They should show love without expecting it to be returned, lend where there is little hope of repayment, and give without reserve or limit. Indeed, they should do good to those who hate them (Luke 6:27-36). The basis for such radical love is found in God's love, who sent his own Son to demonstrate his love for the world (John 3:16). Surprisingly, in John's gospel the term "world" is not simply a casual reference to planet earth or to its inhabitants, but rather a technical term that refers to the realm of darkness, which includes all those opposed to God and to God's realm of light; it is that "world" that God loves.

In the New Testament, love is the law of the new order. In fact, those who love others are said to fulfill the law of God (Rom 13:8; Gal 5:14). This love is the work of faith, demanded by it, made possible by it, and counted for righteousness on account of it. Yet Paul is emphatic that love does not originate in the human heart, for it is a divine gift, given to the believer by the Holy Spirit. This gift is to be exercised now, in response to God's gracious act in the death and resurrection of Christ and as a sign of the future consummation of that new creation which God has begun in Christ, a fulfillment that is expected in hope (Rom 5:5).

Love is the primary term describing the result of faith both for the believer and the community in Christ. Because Christ has died and the Holy Spirit has given the community the gift of love, Paul writes that the "love of Christ urges us on" (2 Cor 5:14), controlling us. In the New Testament, human love is said to originate in God's love, for "God is love" (1 John 4:8). This concept, Christianity's outstanding contribution to world theology and exemplified in Christ, is the reason Jesus gives his followers new marching orders, based on his example: "I give you a new commandment, that you love one another. Just as I have loved you, you also should love one another. By this everyone will know that you are my disciples, if you have love for one another" (John 13:34–35).

In Romans 8:18–39 Paul indicates that love provides personal assurance that in everything God works for good for those who love God, meaning that nothing in creation will be able to separate us from the love of God. For Paul and for Christians in general, the eternal love of God becomes in the love of Christ both the decisive reality in our existence and a world-changing event. Indeed, the work of love is God's goal from the beginning of time.

Questions for Discussion and Reflection

Select one or more of the following questions and write your answer(s) in a journal. If you are in a group study, be prepared to share your answers with those in the group.

1. If Christian anthropology begins with original blessing and not original sin, how should we view "sin"? The text speaks of sin as "spiritual nearsightedness" or "moral myopia." Does this understanding downplay the role of sin? If so, what metaphor would you use to define sin's role in social and human life?
2. The theological virtues are considered to be "gifts" as well as "virtues." Explain the similarities between these concepts, as well as the key distinction between them.
3. In your own words, explain the role of faith in spiritual transformation. If faith is said to be related to the intellect, what is the first step in the renewal of one's mind?
4. In your own words, explain the interconnectedness of faith and hope.
5. In your own words, explain the role of hope in spiritual transformation.
6. If human love is said to come from divine love, how are these two forms of love similar and how are they different?
7. Augustine defined love as "a movement of the soul toward enjoying God for God's own sake." Practically speaking, how does one go about "enjoying God for God's own sake"?

The Theological Virtues

8. Augustine famously described the members of the Trinity metaphorically, using the analogy of love. To the best of your ability, explain Augustine's approach, assessing its usefulness as a way to understand the mystery of the Holy Trinity. Can you think of other analogies that effectively convey the Christian experience of the Trinity?

9. How would you characterize God's love for Israel in the Old Testament?

10. How would you characterize God's love for humanity in the New Testament?

11. If love is said to be related to the human attribute of emotion, what is the first step in the renewal of one's heart?

14

Returning the Church to Its Roots

EVERY VERSE OF THE New Testament presupposes the new people of God, a new community called the church. From the beginning, Christians were described as "the body of Christ," followers of Jesus who showed by their lifestyle that they were a part of the new order that Jesus had announced and that they believed had now arrived. Theologically, the church was a microcosm of the transformation that God's new order would bring for the whole world. To be in the church was to have a foretaste of life as God's new people. Socially, the church in the Roman Empire was an alternative society, based not on selfishness and greed and exploitation, but on the new freedom and fellowship that Jesus had announced: freedom to love God and to love and serve others (Mark 12:29–31). As the church expanded across the Mediterranean world, it was indeed a new society—a context in which people of diverse social, racial, and religious backgrounds were united in a new and radical friendship. Because they had been reconciled to God, they found themselves reconciled to each other.

Jesus conceived his mission to be that of calling the remnant of Israel—twelve disciples, corresponding to the twelve-tribe structure of Israel—to covenant faithfulness. And when the meaning of Jesus' life, death, and resurrection came upon these disciples with overwhelming power at the festival of Pentecost (Acts 2), a powerful movement emerged, rightly termed the Age of the Spirit. This small community became a dynamic and militant church, with a message that "turned the world upside down" (Acts 17:6) and a gospel that was carried enthusiastically to the ends of the earth. The Acts of the Apostles gives the story of the emerging church.

The expansion was amazingly rapid. Within ten years of the death of Jesus, there were Christian communities throughout Palestine and Syria; in twenty years, across Asia Minor and into Greece; and in twenty-five years, in Rome.

Christian expansion, as narrated in the book of Acts, resulted in a twofold shift: geographically, the center of the church gravitated from Jerusalem to Rome; ethnically, the church's identity shifted from Jewish Christians to predominantly Gentile Christians. According to Acts, the church expanded because it fulfilled faithfully its two tasks in society: to evangelize, that is, to serve as Christ's witnesses "to the ends of the earth" (Acts 1:8; see also Matthew's Great Commission in 28:19-20), and to live by the ethics of love and mercy that Jesus had taught.

While stressing the newness of the church, we must also keep in mind the relation of this community to the entire Old Testament heritage. The Old Testament narrates how a people was formed to be the bearer of God's purpose in history and the instrument of God's saving work. Israel was not primarily a race or a nation but a covenant community created by God's action. Having delivered Israel from slavery in Egypt, God made them a covenant people. Through many tumultuous years, God educated and disciplined them in order that they might understand more deeply the meaning of their special role.

It was Second Isaiah who understood most profoundly Israel's place in God's worldwide purpose. According to this prophet, Israel was called to be a "light to the nations" (Isa 49:6) and a servant whose sufferings would benefit all humanity (Isa 49:3; 53:4-6, 11-12). However, in the intervening years, this expansive vision was obscured. The last two centuries before Jesus witnessed a resurgence of Jewish nationalism that led in time to wars with Rome. In 70 CE the Romans destroyed the temple, leveled Jerusalem, and removed the last vestiges of Jewish statehood.

Thus, in the fullness of time, God acted once again to reconstitute the community of Israel—no longer bound by ethnic or nationalistic limitations but open to all people, Jew and Gentile alike, on the basis of faith. The new community did not establish a clean break with the people of God whose life story is portrayed in the Old Testament. Rather, as Paul puts it in his important discussion in Romans 9-11, the community is a "remnant chosen by grace." It is, so to speak, a "wild olive shoot" grafted onto the olive tree (Israel); and the "branch" (Gentile Christians) is supported by the

Christlikeness

roots that reach down deeply into God's choice of Israel and God's faithful dealings with this people (Rom 11:17–24).

Though the early church regarded itself as the true Israel, outwardly it differed little from the numerous synagogues that existed in Jerusalem. Like other members of the synagogues, its members took part in the regular worship of the temple (Luke 24:53; Acts 2:46; 3:1), observed the Jewish festivals, and in general kept the Mosaic law. Although some parallels can be drawn with the ancient Hebrew temple observances, the church in the New Testament was more similar to the Jewish synagogue (a learning center) than to the temple and its cultic activities. The first Christians, themselves Jews or proselytes to Judaism, modeled church worship after synagogue worship. This pattern included readings from scripture, prayer, preaching, and singing. The service closed with a distinctively Christian addition, the breaking of bread (the Lord's Supper or Eucharist), the central mystery at the heart of Christianity (see Acts 2:42). At first, homes of believers served as the places of worship; only later did Christians build church structures comparable to Jewish synagogues. The cross became the central cultic object, rather than the Ark of the Covenant or Torah scrolls. The cross served as a sign of Jesus' crucifixion and resurrection and symbolized the meaning of these events. The first day of the week (Sunday), which commemorated Jesus' resurrection, replaced the Jewish Sabbath as the primary cultic season. In addition to the regular activities of worship and education, which helped to unify the new Christian community, the basic cultic acts were baptism and the Lord's Supper.

Such worship and religious practices did not emerge without problems, however, and new leaders were required. Initially, the disciples of Jesus (the Twelve) became prominent leaders of the Jerusalem church, with a smaller number—consisting of Peter, John, and James "the Just"—exercising greater influence. A somewhat larger group, known as apostles, became the preeminent figures in the spread of Christianity. This group included the Twelve, but the total company of apostles was more numerous. What made a person an apostle was a personal commission by Jesus (the Greek word *apostolos* means "one sent"). Apostles were ambassadors of the risen Lord, understood to have extraordinary authority in the church.

In the world beyond Jerusalem, the church generally assumed the form of a synagogue, that is, a congregation. The Greek word for church (*ekklēsia*) means a group of people called together. It is one of the words used in the Septuagint to designate the assembly of the people of Israel. Because the Jews chose the word *synagogē* for their assemblies, it is quite likely that the first Christians deliberately, and to avoid confusion, rejected the term adopted by the Jews and chose the other. Almost from the start, church congregations were governed by elders (Greek, *presbuteros*), one of whom was chief. With the passage of time, the office of chief elder evolved into that of bishop. Ephesians 4:11 lists prophets, evangelists, pastors, and teachers after apostles among the spiritually gifted leaders of the early church. Apostles stand first in 1 Corinthians 12:28, followed by prophets, teachers, miracle workers, healers, helpers, administrators, speakers in tongues, and interpreters. In keeping with the order of both lists, Paul assigned particular honor to the office of prophet (see 1 Cor 14:1–19). While the authority of the apostle was derived from a connection with Jesus, that of the church prophet was entirely charismatic. As the church developed, the authority of the apostles was passed from the apostles to the bishops through apostolic succession, an authority initially not concerned with the passing of power but of correct teaching. Over time the charismatic offices in the church waned, whereas apostolic authority was deemed irreplaceable.

As developed by Paul, the church presupposes a faith community that is the source of social unity. All life, whether politics, economics, education, or religion, stands under the covenant relation to God. Within that conception, every believer has a part to play. Whether Christians meet together for worship or fellowship, all members are indispensable for all have something to contribute (see 1 Cor 14:26–33). As a result, Paul asserts that every Christian has a distinct *charism*, a ministry that is not restricted by either ordination or some other special experience, but which is given to all by the work of the Spirit in the lives of believers (1 Cor 12:7).

In the church, all members are of equal importance, and that includes equality of women with men. Because Paul's letters contain conflicting statements about the place of women in the church's life (due in part to later editorial activity), the recommended starting place for discussing Paul's own view is Galatians 3:28: "There is no longer Jew or Greek, there is no longer slave or free, there is no longer male and female; for all of you are one in Christ." Despite statements to the contrary, generally seen as interpolations (see 1 Cor 14:33b–36) or post-Pauline (see 1 Tim 2:11–15), the early Christian movement clearly affirmed sexual equality, prompting Thomas Cahill to call the primitive church "the world's first egalitarian society." Likewise, Cahill declares Paul's statement in 1 Corinthians 11:11 (that "in the Lord woman is not independent of man or man independent

Christlikeness

of woman") to be the clearest affirmation of sexual equality in the entire Bible—indeed, the first in world literature.[1] Paul happily worked alongside women, some of whom were his close friends (Phil 4:2–3). His most extensive list of greetings to Christian leaders includes many women (Rom 16:1–15), and he refers to at least one of them as "apostle" (Junia, Rom 16:7). Furthermore, when Paul advises the church at Corinth about the appropriate way to behave, he takes it for granted that both men and women should pray or prophecy in public worship (1 Cor 11:4–5). In 1 Corinthians 11:1–16 Paul uses rabbinic arguments where it suits him, moving in two directions simultaneously: conserving tradition by upholding the custom of head-covering, yet breaking with tradition in allowing women to participate in worship. The whole frame of reference is determined by Paul's insistence that men and women have the same freedom and opportunity to play a full part in the life of the church.

The same point also comes out clearly when Paul discusses marriage in 1 Corinthians 7. Some of what he writes is obscure, no doubt because of its specific reference to details of the Corinthian situation. However, the general principle is clear: Men and women relate to each other not through domination but by mutual love and service.

For Paul what determines a person's function in the church is the endowment of God's Spirit. In God's new society, social distinctions such as gender, race, and social class are irrelevant. The heart of the gospel is freedom: freedom from guilt, from the Law, from sin, and from all that would inhibit the development of one's God-given potential. To be set free by Christ is to be released into a new world in which people can find their own true identity, relating to each other in freedom and fellowship because they are related to Christ himself. The final transformation, however, is yet in the future, when the "glorious freedom of the children of God" will be fully realized (Rom 8:21). In the meantime, the church stands as a testimony to that future hope, and as the context in which people can serve one another as they love and serve God.

The earliest church was undoubtedly charismatic. These early believers were dominated by their experience of the Holy Spirit at work among them, so they gave little thought to the problems of organizing the infant church. They believed the Holy Spirit was the only organizing force they needed. This understanding of Christian fellowship became central for Paul and quite likely for other apostles as well. The authentic picture of a

---

1. Cahill, *Desire of the Everlasting Hills*, 148.

church in the New Testament is of groups of Christians acting together in a spirit of mutual love and friendship. When Paul wrote to the church at Rome some twenty years after the events at Pentecost, there seems to have been no organized hierarchy. Yet over the next century, even within the next half-century, this changed dramatically.

The New Testament church was not a perfect body. In 1 Corinthians, Paul addresses many flaws, among them sectarianism, divisiveness, perfectionism, superiority, insincerity, arrogance, immorality, liturgical improprieties, and eucharistic malpractice. Paul rebukes some members, while condemning sinful behavior. Further dissension appeared later in the apostolic churches, mainly over "false teaching." Nevertheless, the emphasis is on unity, particularly in essentials. In worship, secular and social distinctions were to be abolished (Gal 3:28; Philem 16), although women were kept subservient to men, at least in some of the churches (1 Cor 14:34; 1 Tim 2:11–12).

While inequality is condemned, there was apparently no advocacy yet for the liberation of slaves. Many Christians, in fact, were slaves, for in the Roman Empire slavery was the foundation on which the entire economic structure of society rested. Slavery, as we know, was so ingrained in ancient imperial societies that it would take some eighteen hundred years before abolition was addressed. New Testament church members were drawn from all levels of society. Some, having positions of importance in the secular community, were wealthy enough to own slaves and to have houses large enough for meetings to be held there. But these were a minority.

From the start, one serious problem threatened the church's survival: the terms on which Gentiles could become Christians. At first, it was unclear whether Gentiles should be required to keep the Old Testament laws, either in whole or in part (Acts 10:1—11:18; 15:1–35; Gal 2:1-10). In the end, however, Gentiles were accepted without on the grounds that Jew and Gentile had been reconciled to one another through the death of Christ (Eph 2:13–18). Christ is the vine, they are the branches (John 15:1–11); the church is the olive tree, to which the natural branches (Israel) have been grafted and the wild branches (Gentiles) engrafted. God's work of election, as Paul and other early Christian writers stressed, is not based on ethnicity, gender, or merit but on grace.

When we examine the role and identity of the modern church, we find it is primary designed to promote and support the sin-salvation or atonement-doctrinal paradigm of Christianity. While this ecclesiastical

Christlikeness

model was developed and perfected under Roman patronage, it underwent modification during the Reformation, when Anabaptists (Radical Reformers) challenged the notion of the "territorial church" (in which individuals are required to join local/regional congregations) by adhering to the notion of the "gathered church" (in which individuals are free to join congregations of their choice).

While the influence of the church in the Western world has changed significantly since the 1950s, due in part to growing secularization and rapid decline in membership, the church continues to play a vital role in the lives of millions of people around the world. Over the years, however, the church has changed dramatically in organization from the first community of disciples and ensuing local faith communities meeting primarily in homes to regional groups and later to formal hierarchical bodies mirroring authoritative institutions of the Roman and Byzantine empires.

Over the last five hundred years (particularly as a result of the Protestant Reformation), the church has also experienced "downward mobility," meaning it has expressed itself in less hierarchical, less centralized, and less imperial forms, thereby recapturing its earlier plurality of forms.

During his ministry, Jesus modeled a "small team" or "small group" approach to what we might call "Christian faith, life, and worship." While he did not neglect communal worship (he occasionally visited synagogues in Galilee as well as the temple in Jerusalem) his spirituality was fed by private worship and by a way of life revolving around the cultivation of a small band of disciples. As far as we know, Jesus used a "family approach" to spiritual life and worship. He did not limit spirituality or ministry to set days or times of the week, but pursued it as a way of life. While most people are not called to imitate Jesus' way of life, all are called to follow him, and the best way to do so is through "small group" ministry. This doesn't mean that Christians should stop worshipping in large churches, but what I am suggesting is that if you attend a large church, find a small group within that congregation with which to identify, minister, and grow, whether it be a study group, a group focused on a specific cause or designed to meet specific social and spiritual needs, or both.

Instead of regarding small groups or congregations as separate from the main body of Christians, why not embrace them and celebrate diversity? What if the Christian faith was meant to exist in a variety of forms rather than in an imperial one? When the church exists in many forms rather than in one form, it can be more nimble, less rigid and static, and more responsive to the Holy Spirit.

If, instead of arguing about which ecclesiastical form is correct or legitimate, wouldn't it be far better if we see ourselves as servants of a grand mission, advocates of a great vision, and seekers on a common quest? And what if, instead of focusing on what we are saved *from*, we focus on what we are saved *for*?

Of the many possible models to the Christian quest, there is one that continually beckons us, both with its depth and its simplicity, namely, that the church exists "to form Christlike people, people of Christlike love."[2] This unifying vision of forming Christlike people of love requires a profound openness to the Holy Spirit. It is not our effort that accomplishes this, but rather our willingness to embody a Christ-following, God-loving way of life passed on through our churches.

In this respect, we embrace the Bible as God's Word not because it is God's rulebook or God's answer book, but because the Bible reveals Jesus, whose message and way of life revolved around an ethic of love based on the command to love God and others as self. Just as the Bible does not exist as a sacred constitution to be followed literally or verbatim but rather as a guide and stimulus to energize our spirituality, vision, and mission, so also Jesus did not come to be the object of Christian worship but rather to reveal God's will and nature.

As the Quaker scholar Elton Trueblood often told his student, the Christian doctrine of the divinity of Christ does not simply mean that Jesus is like God. Rather, it means that God is like Jesus. This concept is so powerful and groundbreaking that I encourage you to stop and ponder its meaning. While initially such teaching might seem distracting, perplexing, or even mistaken, it is startlingly true. The incarnation of Jesus does not mean that he came to fit a set of predetermined doctrines or categories concerning his deity. Instead, Jesus came to bring us a new definition or understanding of God. Thus, to experience God in Jesus requires a new understanding of God. This means that the character of Jesus provides us with a unique and indispensable guide and the highest, deepest, and most mature view of the character of the living God.

Several passages of the New Testament make this quite clear. In Colossians, for example, we read that Jesus is "the image of the invisible God . . .

---

2. The topic of Christlikeness here is adopted from McLaren, *New Kind of Christianity*, 164–72.

Christlikeness

For in him the fullness of God was pleased to dwell" (1:15, 19). Likewise, in Hebrews we read that Jesus is "the reflection of God's glory and the exact imprint of God's very being" (1:3), and in John's gospel Jesus tells his disciples that "Whoever has seen me has seen the Father" (14:9).

In 1 Corinthians, Paul introduces the concept of love by speaking of spiritual gifts, that is, of gifts the Spirit of God gives all believers, not for personal or sectarian advantage, but for the "common good." Composed of many parts, the church of Jesus Christ is one body (12:12–13). Each part is essential; furthermore, each part belongs to the others (12:15–20) and needs the others (12:21–24). God's goal is that there be robust diversity without division. In addition to being "the church of God" (1:2) and the temple of the Holy Spirit (3:16–17), the church is also the body or embodiment of Christ (12:27).

After speaking of the diversity of gifts and of the need of using them for the common good, Paul exhorts believers to strive for the "greater gifts" (12:31), of which the greatest is love (13:13). While love is central to all spiritual gifts—essential to the gift of knowledge, of faith, healing, working of miracles, prophecy, discernment, spiritual language, or interpretation of spiritual mysteries (12:8–10), without love, they are useless (13:1–3), for there is no spiritual maturity without love. In fact, in comparison with love, all other methods, goals, and activities seem childish, a partial reflection in a dirty mirror (13:11–12). Those who love unconditionally, with God's agape love, become Christlike, and to be Christlike is to know and see God intimately, "face to face" (13:12). For Paul, such love, such knowing and seeing, is consummated in eternal glory.

In 1 Corinthians, as in all scripture and in all knowing and living, love has the last word (16:14). The church, like life itself, must be above all a school of love, for in this school God trains Christlike people, people who live in the way of peacemaking, the way of the kingdom of God, and the way of the Spirit. The school of love is the future of the church, which means the church of the future will be a school of listening, dialogue, reconciliation, mature inquiry, and understanding. This way of wisdom will be prophetic, generous, inclusive, compassionate, equitable, and nondualist, and it will be led by women and men of all cultures, races, and social classes, themselves caught in the lifelong and divine process of personal and social transformation.

If the current wineskins were developed and molded to serve the old wine of Platonic-Roman, tribal, hierarchical, non-kingdom of God types of Christianity, in all likelihood they will be replaced by new wineskins fit for the one mission that truly matters: forming people of Christlike love. Ultimately, the church's mission is to create a "grace space" in which the Spirit works to form Christlike people.[3] When that happens, God's will will be done on earth as in heaven (see Matt 6:10), for heaven will have come down upon us and God's eternal and unconditional love will be manifest in word and deed. To understand what Christlikeness looks like in action, we need only read and ponder Paul's description in 1 Corinthians 13:4–7: "Love is patient; love is kind; love is not envious or boastful or arrogant or rude. It does not insist on its own way; it is not irritable or resentful; it does not rejoice in wrongdoing, but rejoices in the truth. It bears all things, believes all things, hopes all things, endures all things."

Such love—such Christlikeness—"never ends."

Questions for Discussion and Reflection

Select one or more of the following questions and write your answer(s) in a journal. If you are in a group study, be prepared to share your answers with those in the group.

1. After reading this chapter, what qualities in the early church marked this institution as God's new order for the world?

2. In your estimation, why did the early church expand so rapidly in the Gentile world? By comparison, what explanation do you give for the decrease in size and influence of the modern Western church? In your estimation, can the current shift be reversed? If so, what needs to happen for the church to experience outward growth and expansion?

3. If the early church considered itself a branch (a "wild olive shoot") of Judaism, what does this say about current Jewish-Christian relations? Should modern Christians work toward reconciliation with Jews? Why or why not?

4. In your estimation, should or must today's church be hierarchical and authoritarian, or be more egalitarian? If possible, chart out a model of your ideal church and its leadership.

---

3. I am indebted to the Rev. Dr. Joan Prentice and her leadership team at The Ephesus Project in Pittsburgh for use of this marvelous term to describe Christlikeness in faith, worship, and action.

Christlikeness

5. If the early church affirmed sexual or gender equality, why did the church discontinue this practice?
6. In your estimation, what role must God's Spirit play in modern church belief and practice? Explain your answer.
7. In your estimation, what is the difference between "true" and "false" teaching in the church? In this respect, which has primacy, theology (belief) or ethics (practice)? Explain your answer.
8. Explain the merit or benefits of the "small team" or "small group" approach to Christian life and worship.
9. In your estimation, what role should the Bible play in modern Christian life and worship?
10. Explain what Elton Trueblood meant when he taught that Christianity emphasizes that God is like Jesus rather than that Jesus is like God.
11. Explain the meaning of the author's statement that in all knowing and living, love has the last word.

Bibliography

Anderson, Bernhard W. *Understanding the Old Testament*. 5th ed. Upper Saddle River, NJ: Pearson Prentice Hall, 2007.

Armstrong, Karen. *A History of God*. New York: Ballantine, 1993.

Becker, Lawrence. *A New Stoicism*. Princeton, NJ: Princeton University Press, 2017.

Benedict XVI, Pope. *Spe Salvi*. Rome: Libreria Editrice Vaticana, 2007. w2.vatican.va/content/benedict-xvi/en/encyclicals/documents/hf_ben-xvi_enc_20071130_spe-salvi.html.

Borg, Marcus J. *The God We Never Knew*. San Francisco: HarperSanFrancisco, 1998.

———. *The Heart of Christianity: Rediscovering a Life of Faith*. San Francisco: HarperSanFrancisco, 2003.

———. *Meeting Jesus Again for the First Time*. San Francisco: HarperSanFrancisco, 1995.

———. *Reading the Bible Again for the First Time*. San Francisco: HarperSanFrancisco, 2002.

Borg, Marcus, and N. T. Wright. *The Meaning of Jesus: Two Visions*. San Francisco: HarperSanFrancisco, 2000.

Bourgeault, Cynthia. *The Holy Trinity and the Law of Three*. Boston, Shambhala, 2013.

Bradley, Marion Zimmer. *The Mists of Avalon*. New York: Knopf, 1982.

Bregman, Jay. "Logismos and Pistis." In *Pagan and Christian Anxiety: A Response to E. R. Dodds*, edited by Robert C. Smith and John Lounibos, 217–31. New York, University Press of America, 1984.

Brown, Raymond, et al. *The New Jerome Biblical Commentary*. Upper Saddle River, NJ: Prentice Hall, 1990.

Cahill, Thomas. *Desire of the Everlasting Hills*. New York: Anchor, 2001.

Cox, Harvey. *The Future of Faith*. New York: HarperOne, 2009.

Crenshaw, James L. *Old Testament Wisdom: An Introduction*. Atlanta: John Knox, 1981.

Dodds, E. R. *Pagan & Christian in an Age of Anxiety*. New York: Norton, 1970.

Ehrman, Bart D. *A Brief Introduction to the New Testament*. 3rd ed. New York: Oxford University Press, 2013.

———. *Lost Christianities: The Battle for Scripture and the Faith We Never Knew*. New York: Oxford University Press, 2003.

Esposito, John Esposito, et al. *World Religions Today*. New York: Oxford University Press, 2001.

Fowden, Garth. *The Egyptian Hermes: A Historical Approach to the Late Pagan Mind*. Princeton: Princeton University Press, 1988.

Bibliography

Gager, John. *The Origin of Anti-Semitism: Attitudes toward Judaism in Pagan and Christian Antiquity.* New York: Oxford University Press, 1983.

Gordis, Robert. *The Book of God and Man: A Study of Job.* Chicago: The University of Chicago Press, 1965.

Head, Constance. *The Emperor Julian.* Boston: G. K. Hall, 1976.

Heine, Ronald E. *Origen: Scholarship in the Service of the Church.* Oxford: Oxford University Press, 2010.

Hovland, C. Warren, "The Dialogue Between Origen and Celsus." In *Pagan and Christian Anxiety: A Response to E. R. Dodds,* edited by Robert C. Smith and John Lounibos, 191–216. New York, University Press of America, 1984.

Hurtado, Larry W. *One God, One Lord: Early Christian Devotion and Ancient Jewish Monotheism.* Philadelphia: Fortress, 1988.

Inwood, Brad. *The Cambridge Companion to the Stoics.* Cambridge: Cambridge University Press, 2003.

Irvine, William. *A Guide to the Good Life: The Ancient Art of Stoic Joy.* Oxford: Oxford University Press, 2009.

Jonas, Hans. *The Gnostic Religion: The Message of the Alien God and the Beginnings of Christianity.* Boston: Beacon, 1958.

Kee, Howard Clark, et al. *Christianity: A Social and Cultural History.* 2nd ed. Upper Saddle River, NJ: Prentice Hall, 1998.

Klauck, Hans-Joseph. *The Religious Context of Early Christianity: A Guide to Greco-Roman Religions.* Philadelphia: Fortress, 2003.

Lane, Eugene, and Ramsey MacMullen. *Paganism and Christianity: 100–425 CE: A Sourcebook.* 3rd ed. Philadelphia: Fortress, 2005.

Lane Fox, Robin. *Pagan and Christian.* New York: Alfred A. Knopf, 1987.

Lee, A. D. *Pagans and Christians in Late Antiquity: A Sourcebook.* New York: Routledge, 2000.

Lounibos, John. "Plotinus: Pagan, Mystic, Philosopher." In *Pagan and Christian Anxiety: A Response to E. R. Dodds,* edited by Robert C. Smith and John Lounibos, 131–66. New York, University Press of America, 1984.

Maxwell, Jaclyn. *The Oxford Handbook of Late Antiquity.* New York: Oxford University Press, 2012.

McLynn, Neil. *Being Christian in Late Antiquity.* New York: Oxford University Press, 2014.

Lewis, C. S. *The Abolition of Man.* New York: Macmillan, 1947.

Lovin, Robin W. *Christian Ethics: An Essential Guide.* Nashville, TN: Abingdon, 2000.

McLaren, Brian. *A New Kind of Christianity: Ten Questions that are Transforming the Faith.* New York: HarperOne, 2010.

———. *The Secret Message of Jesus: Uncovering the Truth that Could Change Everything.* Nashville, TN: W Publishing, 2006.

Moltmann, Jürgen. *Theology of Hope.* New York: Harper & Row, 1967.

Morris, Rudolph E. *The Fathers of the Church: A New Translation 7.* Washington, DC: Catholic University of America Press, 1970.

O'Connor, Kathleen M. *The Wisdom Literature.* Collegeville, MN: Liturgical, 1990.

O'Donnell, James J. *Pagans: The End of Traditional Religion and the Rise of Christianity.* New York: Ecco, 2016.

Pigliucci, Massimo. *A Field Guide to a Happy Life: 53 Brief Lessons for Living.* New York: Basic Books, 2020.

Bibliography

———. *How to Be a Stoic: Using Ancient Philosophy to Live a Modern Life*. New York: Basic Books, 2017.

Polkinghorne, John. *Quarks, Chaos, & Christianity: Questions to Science and Religion*. New York: Crossroad, 1998.

Rivers, James. *Religion in the Roman Empire*. Malden, MA: Wiley-Blackwell, 2006.

Robertson, Donald. *Stoicism and the Art of Happiness: Practical Wisdom for Everyday Life*. London, England: Teach Yourself, 2018.

Royalty, Robert M. *The Origin of Heresy: A History of Discourse in Second Temple Judaism and Early Christianity*. London: Routledge, 2012.

Rudolph, Kurt. *Gnosis: The Nature and History of Gnosticism*. San Francisco: HarperOne, 1987.

Schulweis, Harold M. *For Those Who Can't Believe*. New York: HarperPerennial, 1995.

Sellers, John. *Stoicism*. Berkeley, CA: University of California Press, 2006.

Smith, Robert C., and John Lounibos. *Pagan and Christian Anxiety: A Response to E. R. Dodds*. New York, University Press of America, 1984.

Spong, John Shelby. *A New Kind of Christianity for a New World*. New York: HarperOne, 2001.

———. *Liberating the Gospels: Reading the Bible with Jewish Eyes*. San Francisco: HarperSanFrancisco, 1996.

———. *Rescuing the Bible from Fundamentalism*. San Francisco: HarperSanFrancisco, 1991.

———. *The Sins of Scripture*. New York: HarperOne, 2006.

———. *Why Christianity Must Change or Die*. New York: HarperOne, 1999.

Vande Kappelle, Robert. *The Arc of Spirituality: The Western Love Affair with God*. Eugene, OR: Wipf & Stock, 1921.

———. *Beyond Belief*. Eugene, OR: Wipf & Stock, 2012.

———. *The Church Alumni Association: A Handbook for Believers in Exile*. Eugene, OR: Wipf & Stock, 2021.

———. *Dark Splendor: Spiritual Fitness for the Second Half of Life*. Eugene, OR: Resource, 2015.

———. *Living Graciously on Planet Earth: Faith, Hope, and Love in Biblical, Social, and Cosmic Context*. Eugene, OR: Wipf & Stock, 2016.

———. *The New Creation: Church History Made Accessible, Relevant, and Personal*. Eugene, OR: Wipf & Stock, 2018.

———. *Outgrowing Cultic Christianity: Restoring the Role of Religion*. Eugene, OR: Wipf & Stock, 2021.

———. *Refined by Fire: Essential Teachings in Scripture*. Eugene, OR: Wipf & Stock, 2018.

———. *Response to the Other: Jews and Christians in an Age of Paganism*. Eugene, OR: Wipf & Stock, 2020.

———. *The Second Journey: Visions and Voices on First- and Second-Half-of-Life-Spirituality*. Eugene, OR: Wipf & Stock, 2020.

———. *Securing Life: The Enduring Message of the Bible*. Eugene, OR: Wipf & Stock, 2016.

Wright, Robert. *The Evolution of God*. New York: Little, Brown, 2009.

Index

Aelius Aristides, 86–87
afterlife, belief in, 56, 67, 79, 86, 147
Albright, William, 42–43, 44
animism, 25, 38
Anselm of Canterbury, 141
apatheia (indifference), 73, 123
Apollonius of Tyana, 84, 93, 94
apologetic literature, 96–100
apologia, 90
Apostles' Creed, 98
Apuleius, 87
Aquinas, Thomas, 5, 19, 24, 33, 62, 115, 116, 118, 119, 120, 130, 150, 159
arête, 116, 128
Aristotle, Aristotelianism, 33, 64, 67, 68, 70, 71–72, 93, 96, 99, 110, 111, 112, 113, 114, 115, 116, 118, 124, 125, 127, 128, 137n1, 142
Asclepius (deity), 86, 94, 103
atheism, 15, 25, 29, 38, 65, 81, 103, 132
Augustine of Hippo, 3, 19, 33, 62, 90, 103, 104, 107, 130, 159, 160

Bacharach, Burt, 159
Barth, Karl, 24
Basil of Caesarea, 143
Beard, Charles A., 52
beauty, 6, 68, 71, 75, 76, 77
bibliolatry, 16–17
Blumhardt, Christoph Friedrich, 14
Borg, Marcus, 25, 26, 27
Bourgeault, Cynthia, 5n4
Boy Scouts, 4
Bradley, Marion Zimmer, 30
Brown, Brené, 32

Cahill, Thomas, 167
Calvin, Calvinism, 17, 19, 154
Carey, William, 143
Cato the Younger, 140
Celsus, 90, 91–92, 95, 99, 103, 106
Christendom, 9, 14, 15, 17, 30, 36, 111, 112, 113
Christian(s), 2, 3, 8, 10, 14, 16, 17, 18, 28, 31, 33, 36, 77, 108
Christian-pagan debate, 89–108
Christianity, 4, 8, 9, 13, 14, 17, 30, 32, 36, 62, 75, 76, 108, 114
    Greco-Roman roots of, 62–64, 113
    Jewish roots of, 37–60, 62, 66, 80–81, 89, 102, 111, 112, 165–66, 169
    as personal philosophy, 13, 20
    as religion, 13, 14, 26, 35
Christlikeness, 8, 171, 173
Chrysippus, 128, 133
church, 9, 10, 14, 15, 35, 36, 87, 108, 164–73
    as "catholic," 33
Cicero, 115, 132
Clement of Alexandria, 33, 73, 89, 91, 92, 93, 104, 105, 106
Constantine (emperor), 9, 15, 16, 30, 94, 113, 130
cosmopolitanism, 130, 137, 139, 141, 145
courage, 73, 104, 107, 116, 117, 119, 128, 140, 150, 157, 158
Cox, Harvey, 113
Cynic, Cynicism, 64, 65, 124
Cyprian, 93

Index

daimonia, 84, 87
Dante Alighieri, 140
Darwin, Charles, 38
David, Hal, 159
Decius, 93
Descartes, René, 75, 130
determinism, 131, 133–34, 146
Diocletian, 94, 103
Diogenes of Sinope, 65
discipleship, 7–8, 153
divination, 146
Dodds, E. R., 103
dualism, dualistic, 5n4, 18, 19, 20, 24, 29, 31, 32, 57, 68, 70, 71, 72, 110, 111, 112, 113

Emerson, Ralph Waldo, 130
Enlightenment, 30, 130
Epictetus, 126, 129, 132, 136, 137, 138, 141
Epicurus, Epicureanism, 64, 65, 130, 146
eschatology, 8, 106, 147, 155–56, 158
ethics
    Christian, 3
    pagan, 83
    Stoic, 123, 133, 145
eudaimonia, eudaimonic, 122, 124, 125, 127, 128, 137
Eusebius, 103
evil, 57, 76, 133, 147

faith, 150, 151–55, 157, 158
fire, 146
fortitude, 5, 117, 119, 120
Friedrich, Georg Wilhelm, 38
fundamentalism, 10, 19

Galen, 90, 91, 103, 104
Girl Scouts, 4
gnostic, gnosticism, 62, 64, 66, 73, 74, 75, 91, 93, 97, 98, 105, 106
God, 2, 19, 37, 38, 96, 129, 136, 156, 157, 158, 171
    belief in, 3, 23
    as Fire, 146
    image of, 19, 143
    in human form, 41
    knowing, 24, 172
    as Light, 72
    love of, 3, 105, 160, 161, 162
    as material being, 72
    models of, 25–28
    as Nature, 132
    nature of, 33, 79, 106
    as the One, 75, 76, 77
    oneness of, 30, 40
    as perfect reason, 72
    as personal being, 23–24, 27, 28, 129
    as Prime Mover (First Cause), 71
    and supernatural theism, 23, 24–25, 29
    titles for, 44–47
    as "Totally Other," 24
Golden Rule, 139, 145
good and evil, 5n4, 59, 133
"good life," 1–4, 54, 116, 123, 126, 150
Great Commandment, 6, 8, 139, 144, 145, 149, 161, 164, 171
Gregory of Nyssa, 106

happiness, 2, 6, 66–67, 72, 128, 136, 144–45
heaven, 104, 105, 106
hell, 105
henotheism, 25, 39, 42
Heraclitus, 33, 68, 99, 123, 132, 133, 146
Hermeticism, 67, 73–74, 77, 104
Hierocles, 95, 129, 137, 139
Holy Bible, 3, 4, 16, 19, 20, 33, 36, 37, 79, 113, 142, 153, 156–58, 160–62, 171
    allegorical reading of, 66, 92, 98, 106
    poetry in, 50
    wisdom literature in, 50–50, 114
Holy Spirit, 6, 14, 17, 26–28, 31, 32, 146, 157, 160, 161, 167, 168, 171, 172
    as *pneuma*, 146
Homer, Homeric, 72, 93, 99, 106, 140
hope, 147, 150, 151, 154–58
Hume, David, 130

indifference. *See apatheia*
Inge, W. R., 99
Irenaeus, 90, 91, 93, 97–98, 105

Index

James, letter of, 56, 145
Jesus Christ, 3, 6, 10, 14, 63–64, 79, 93, 137n1, 155, 161–62
   and church, 170
   as divine, 84–85, 96, 107, 171
   ethical teaching of, 11, 144, 170–71
   following, 7
   and God, 171–72
   as hero, 6, 142–43
   as human, 6–7, 19, 107
   and kenosis, 31
   as Logos, 21, 33, 67, 107, 115, 133
   as Lord, 13
   and nondualism, 146
   as Pantocrator, 17
   and power, 32
   as role model, 13, 141–44
   as sage, 56–57
   as "wisdom of God," 56, 67
Julian (emperor), 90, 95–96, 107
justice, 118–19
Justin Martyr, 90, 91, 97
Justinian (emperor), 16, 107

Kant, Immanuel, 130
Kierkegaard, Søren, 14
kingdom of God, 9, 10, 14, 15, 16, 151, 172

Lewis, C. S., 115
Lipsius, Justus, 131
logismos, 103, 104
love, 6, 30, 150, 151, 158–62, 171, 172, 173
Lovin, Robin, 3
Lucian of Samosata, 91, 103
Luther, Martin, 36

Mandela, Nelson, 143
Marcion, Marcionites, 62, 91, 98
Marcus Aurelius, 86, 90, 103, 125, 129, 130, 147
McLaren, Brian, 8, 9
Mill, John Stuart, 24
Moltmann, Jürgen, 155
monism, 68, 72, 146
monotheism, 11, 29, 37–48, 60, 86, 131, 132, 147
   definition of, 39

Murphy, Roland, 58
Musonius Rufus, 129, 137–39
mystery religions, 85–87, 129

nature, living in harmony with, 137n1
Neoplatonism, 9, 62, 64, 67, 74–77, 90, 92, 94, 95, 99, 104, 107, 111, 113
Neostoicism, 131
Nero (emperor), 94, 137

O'Connor, Kathleen, 57
Odysseus, 140–41
oikeiosis, 139
Origen of Alexandria, 33, 89, 90, 91–93, 95, 97, 98–99, 104–7

pagan, paganism, 15, 18, 64, 81, 82–85
   demise of, 107–8
pagan-Christian debate, 89–108
Panaetius, 128, 129
panentheism, 25, 29
pantheism, 25, 29, 129, 132, 134, 146, 147
Parmenides, 68
Pascal, Blaise, 152
Paul (apostle), 5, 6, 8, 31, 33, 56, 62, 63, 67, 79, 93, 103, 105, 106, 114, 129, 130, 131, 144, 147, 150, 151, 157, 158, 161, 162, 165, 167, 168, 169, 172
Peripatetics, Peripateticism, 124, 125
Philo of Alexandria, 53, 73, 96, 104, 129
philosophy, pagan, 2, 64–77, 104
   and religion, 64
pistis, 103, 104, 107, 153–54
Plato, Platonism, 9, 33, 62, 64, 65, 67, 68–72, 74, 75, 76, 87, 90, 91, 92, 93, 96, 99, 104, 106, 110, 112, 114, 124, 128, 130, 142
Plotinus, 64, 74–77, 91, 92, 93, 104, 105, 110
Plutarch, 87
pneuma, 146
Polkinghorne, John, 152
polytheism, 15, 20, 25, 29, 39, 40, 42, 43, 48, 82, 86, 95, 132
Porphyry, 74, 77, 90, 94, 95, 103, 106, 107–8

Index

Posidonius, 128, 129
prayer, 16, 23, 24, 83, 146, 166
providence, 85, 96, 144, 145, 147
prudence (wisdom), 117–18
Pythagoras, Pythagoreanism, 64, 69, 84, 86, 93, 94

reason, rationality (*logos*), 58, 70, 72, 137n1, 144, 147
Reformation, Reformers, Protestant, 16, 17, 18, 20, 36, 113, 170
religion, 28–29
   in the Greco-Roman world, 81–87
   task of, 10
Renaissance, 18, 130
role ethics, 136–41
   definition of, 136
Rousseau, Jean-Jacques, 130
Russell, Bertrand, 35

salvation, 8, 16, 47, 64, 79, 104, 105, 107, 111, 141, 161, 169, 171
Schulweis, Harold, 24
scripture. *See* Holy Bible
Sellars, John, 131
Seneca, 129, 130, 131, 132, 140, 144, 146, 147
Severus Alexander (emperor), 93, 98
sin, 27–28, 111–12, 147, 149
   original, 8, 112, 141
Smith, Adam, 130
Smith, Morton, 47–48
Socrates, Socratic, 64, 69, 70, 110, 123, 124, 127, 141, 144, 145
soul, 65, 70, 71, 72, 73, 74, 75, 76, 104, 105, 108, 145, 147
   immortality of, 71, 72
Spinoza, Baruch, 130
Spong, John Shelby, 24
Stoic, Stoicism, 21, 62, 64, 65–66, 67, 72–73, 114, 115, 122, 123, 125–27
   and Christianity, 144–47
   and ethics, 72–73
   goal of, 122
   and God (divine reason), 66, 72, 131–34, 144–45, 145–46

   influence of, 129–31
   and Logos, 21, 33, 72, 136, 145
   role ethics in, 136–41, 145
   storyline of, 122–29
syncretism, syncretistic, 18, 20, 30, 35, 36–37, 47–48, 52, 62, 66, 68, 86, 111–12, 113, 114
synthesis. *See* syncretism

temperance, 119–20, 138
Ten Commandments, 41
Teresa, Mother, 144
Tertullian, 90, 91, 93, 97, 99–100, 107
Theodosius (emperor), 15, 16, 95
theology, 30, 133
   definition of, 23
theurgy, 104
Thoreau, David, 130
totemism, 38–39
Trinity, Holy, 5n4, 31, 32, 76, 99, 141, 160
Trueblood, Elton, 171
truth, 30, 32, 69, 70
Tylor, Edward, 38

unitive consciousness, 20

Vatke, Wilhelm, 40
Vincent of Léarins, 32
virtue ethics, 127, 130
virtues, 4
   cardinal, 4, 114–20, 130, 149, 150
   definition of, 117
   theological, 5, 6, 130, 149–62

Warwick, Dionne, 159
Wellhausen, Julius, 38, 39, 40
Whitehead, Alfred North, 25
Wilberforce, William, 143
wisdom literature, Jewish, 50–60
   and spirituality, 57–60

Yahweh, Yahwism, 40, 41, 42, 43, 44–48

Zeno of Citium, 72, 99, 123, 127–28, 132, 133, 138, 146
Zeus (deity), 31, 84, 132, 133

www.ingramcontent.com/pod-product-compliance
Lightning Source LLC
Chambersburg PA
CBHW071830170426
43191CB00046B/1314